Behind the Vision of Doug Cutting

Hadoop's Hidden Journey – Unauthorized

Rina Da Silva

ISBN: 9781779699893
Imprint: Telephasic Workshop
Copyright © 2024 Rina Da Silva.
All Rights Reserved.

Contents

The Early Years   **1**
A Brilliant Mind is Born   1
Career Beginnings   11

The Rise of Hadoop   **25**
Inception of Hadoop   25
Hadoop's Impact on Big Data   37

Beyond Hadoop: Doug Cutting's Contributions   **51**
Evolution of Hadoop   51
Other Notable Projects and Collaborations   64

Challenges and Successes   **79**
Overcoming Technical Obstacles   79
Industry Recognition and Awards   93

The Man Behind the Code   **105**
Doug Cutting's Personality and Character   105
The Future of Data Processing   115

Index   **131**

The Early Years

A Brilliant Mind is Born

Doug's Childhood Influences

Doug Cutting was born into a world that would soon be transformed by technology, yet his early years were steeped in a rich tapestry of influences that shaped his intellect and creativity. Growing up in the 1970s, Doug found himself in an environment where curiosity was not only encouraged but celebrated. His parents, both educators, instilled in him a love for learning that would lay the groundwork for his future innovations.

From a young age, Doug was captivated by the world of science and mathematics. His father, a physicist, often brought home books filled with complex theories and fascinating experiments. One of Doug's earliest memories was of his father demonstrating the principles of physics through simple household experiments, igniting a spark of inquiry in the young boy. This hands-on approach to learning allowed Doug to grasp abstract concepts in a tangible way, fostering a mindset that would later prove invaluable in his programming career.

Moreover, the influence of his mother, a dedicated teacher, cannot be understated. She introduced him to the wonders of literature and critical thinking, often engaging him in discussions about the stories they read together. This early exposure to narrative and analysis honed Doug's ability to think critically and approach problems from multiple angles. It was during these formative years that he learned the importance of perseverance and intellectual curiosity—qualities that would define his approach to technology.

In addition to his academic influences, Doug's childhood was marked by an early fascination with computers. The late 1970s saw the advent of personal computing, and Doug was no exception to the allure of this new technology. At the age of ten, he received his first computer, an Atari 800, which opened up a world of possibilities.

He spent countless hours experimenting with programming, often creating simple games and applications. This hands-on experience was pivotal; it allowed him to see the immediate impact of his code and the joy of creation.

As Doug began to explore the realm of computing, he was particularly inspired by the burgeoning community of computer enthusiasts who frequented local computer clubs. These gatherings were not merely social events; they were vibrant ecosystems of knowledge sharing and collaboration. Doug learned the value of community and mentorship as he interacted with more experienced programmers who were willing to share their insights and expertise. This collaborative spirit would later become a cornerstone of his work in the open-source movement.

The influence of his surroundings extended beyond his family and peers. Doug grew up in a culturally rich environment that embraced innovation and exploration. The San Francisco Bay Area, known for its progressive ideals and technological advancements, provided a backdrop that encouraged creativity and experimentation. The spirit of Silicon Valley was palpable, and young Doug was inspired by the stories of pioneers who were changing the world through technology. This environment fostered a sense of possibility and ambition that would propel him into a future filled with groundbreaking achievements.

In summary, Doug Cutting's childhood was characterized by a confluence of influences that shaped his identity as a programmer and innovator. The encouragement from his family, the early exposure to computing, and the vibrant community of tech enthusiasts all played a critical role in nurturing his intellectual curiosity and creativity. These foundational experiences not only equipped him with the skills necessary for a successful career in technology but also instilled in him a lifelong passion for learning and collaboration. As he ventured into the world of programming, the lessons learned in his formative years would continue to resonate, guiding him on his journey to becoming one of the most influential figures in the tech industry.

The Impact of Education

Education plays a pivotal role in shaping a person's intellect, character, and career trajectory. For Doug Cutting, the impact of his educational experiences was profound, laying the groundwork for his later innovations in the tech industry. This subsection explores how Cutting's education influenced his thinking, creativity, and his eventual contributions to the field of computing.

Foundational Knowledge

Doug Cutting's academic journey began with a solid foundation in the sciences and mathematics. These subjects are crucial for developing logical reasoning and problem-solving skills, which are essential in programming and software development. Research indicates that a strong background in mathematics enhances one's ability to engage in algorithmic thinking and abstraction, both of which are critical in computer science [?].

For instance, Cutting's exposure to mathematical concepts such as set theory and combinatorics would later inform his understanding of data structures and algorithms. The ability to analyze problems quantitatively is a skill that transcends disciplines, and Cutting's early academic focus on these areas equipped him with the tools necessary to tackle complex challenges in software design.

Influence of Higher Education

Cutting pursued higher education at Stanford University, a prestigious institution known for its rigorous computer science program. At Stanford, he was introduced to a diverse array of topics, including artificial intelligence, database systems, and programming languages. This exposure not only broadened his knowledge base but also ignited his passion for innovation in technology.

The importance of a well-rounded education is underscored by the theory of multiple intelligences, proposed by Howard Gardner. This theory posits that individuals possess different kinds of intelligences, which can be nurtured through varied educational experiences [?]. For Cutting, the interdisciplinary approach at Stanford allowed him to cultivate his logical-mathematical intelligence while also fostering creative thinking through exposure to the arts and humanities.

Hands-On Learning and Projects

One of the most significant aspects of Cutting's education was the emphasis on hands-on learning. Engaging in projects and collaborative work during his time at Stanford allowed him to apply theoretical knowledge in practical settings. This experiential learning is supported by Kolb's Experiential Learning Theory, which posits that knowledge is created through the transformation of experience [?].

For example, during his studies, Cutting participated in group projects that required him to develop software solutions for real-world problems. This not only honed his technical skills but also taught him the importance of teamwork and communication in the software development process. The ability to work collaboratively is essential in the tech industry, where projects often involve cross-functional teams.

Mentorship and Networking

Another critical element of Cutting's education was the mentorship he received from professors and industry professionals. Mentorship plays a crucial role in personal and professional development, providing guidance, support, and opportunities for growth. Research shows that mentorship can significantly impact career advancement and job satisfaction [?].

At Stanford, Cutting had the opportunity to connect with influential figures in the tech industry, which helped him build a network that would prove invaluable throughout his career. Networking is particularly important in the technology sector, where relationships can lead to collaborations, job opportunities, and access to resources.

Challenges in Education

While education can provide numerous advantages, it also presents challenges. For Cutting, the competitive nature of Stanford's computer science program meant that he had to navigate a demanding curriculum while balancing various responsibilities. The pressure to excel academically can lead to stress and burnout, a phenomenon documented in educational psychology [?].

Despite these challenges, Cutting's perseverance and dedication to his studies ultimately paid off. The resilience he developed during his educational journey became a cornerstone of his character, enabling him to tackle the obstacles he would later face in his professional life.

Conclusion

In conclusion, the impact of education on Doug Cutting's life cannot be overstated. His foundational knowledge in mathematics and sciences, the diverse and rigorous curriculum at Stanford, hands-on learning experiences, mentorship opportunities, and the challenges he faced all contributed to shaping him into the innovative thinker he is today. Education not only equipped Cutting with the technical skills necessary for programming but also instilled in him the values of collaboration, perseverance, and creativity. As he ventured into the tech industry, these qualities would prove essential in his journey to create Hadoop and revolutionize the way we process and analyze data.

A BRILLIANT MIND IS BORN

Developing an Interest in Computing

From a young age, Doug Cutting exhibited a curiosity that would later fuel his passion for computing. Growing up in a household where technology was both a tool and a subject of fascination, Doug found himself drawn to the world of computers. His early experiences were pivotal in shaping his interest, as he navigated through the intricate landscape of programming and problem-solving.

Early Exposure to Computers

Doug's journey into computing began with the introduction of personal computers in the 1980s. The allure of these machines, capable of performing complex calculations and tasks at remarkable speeds, captivated his imagination. He recalls the first time he encountered a computer: a friend's Apple II. The vibrant graphics, the beeping sounds, and the endless possibilities sparked a fire within him.

Theoretical Foundations

The foundation of Doug's interest can be traced back to key theoretical concepts in computer science. The notion of algorithms, which can be defined as a finite set of instructions to solve a problem, fascinated him. As he delved deeper, he learned about the significance of data structures, such as arrays and linked lists, which provide a means to organize and manipulate data efficiently.

One of the first algorithms Doug encountered was the sorting algorithm. For instance, the Bubble Sort, a simple yet intuitive method, served as an excellent introduction to algorithmic thinking. The Bubble Sort algorithm can be expressed mathematically as follows:

BubbleSort(A) where A is an array of n elements:

1. For $i = 0$ to $n-1$:
2.   For $j = 0$ to $n-i-1$:
3.   If $A[j] > A[j+1]$ then swap $A[j]$ and $A[j+1]$

This algorithm, despite its inefficiency in large datasets, illustrated the fundamental concepts of iteration and comparison—concepts that would become integral to Doug's programming journey.

Hands-On Experience

Doug's interest was further solidified through hands-on experience. He began experimenting with programming languages, starting with BASIC. Writing simple programs to automate tasks and create games allowed him to see the immediate impact of his code. For example, he created a text-based adventure game that required players to navigate through a maze, reinforcing his understanding of control structures such as loops and conditionals.

As he progressed, Doug ventured into more complex languages like C and Java. The transition from high-level languages to low-level programming introduced him to the intricacies of memory management and data manipulation. He learned about pointers in C, a concept that, while challenging, opened a new realm of possibilities for optimizing performance and understanding how computers operate at a fundamental level.

Problem-Solving Mindset

A significant aspect of Doug's development was his approach to problem-solving. He embraced challenges as opportunities for growth. One notable instance was when he faced a particularly difficult bug in his code. Instead of becoming frustrated, he adopted a systematic approach to debugging:

1. Define the problem clearly.
2. Break the problem down into smaller, manageable parts.
3. Test each part independently to isolate the issue.
4. Use print statements to trace the flow of execution.
5. Reflect on the solution and document the process for future reference.

This methodical approach not only helped him resolve the issue but also instilled a lifelong habit of analytical thinking—a trait that would serve him well in his future endeavors.

Influence of Community and Collaboration

Doug's interest in computing also grew through engagement with the programming community. He actively participated in forums and local user groups where he could share knowledge and collaborate on projects. The open-source movement, in particular, resonated with him, emphasizing the importance of community-driven development. This exposure to collaborative coding environments laid the groundwork for his later contributions to significant projects like Hadoop.

In conclusion, Doug Cutting's early interest in computing was fueled by a combination of exposure to technology, theoretical learning, hands-on programming, and a strong problem-solving mindset. These formative experiences not only shaped his skills but also instilled a passion for innovation and collaboration that would define his career. As he continued to explore the vast world of computing, he was unknowingly laying the groundwork for his future as a pioneer in the field of big data.

Early Programming Projects

Doug Cutting's journey into the realm of programming was marked by a series of early projects that not only honed his technical skills but also laid the groundwork for his future innovations. These projects were characterized by a combination of creativity, problem-solving, and an insatiable curiosity that drove him to explore the capabilities of computers.

The First Lines of Code

Doug's initial foray into programming began during his high school years, where he was introduced to the world of BASIC. This simple yet powerful language allowed him to write his first programs, which included a text-based adventure game that captured the imagination of his peers. The experience of creating interactive narratives sparked a passion for programming that would stay with him throughout his career.

$$\text{Adventure}(x) = \begin{cases} \text{Explore Cave} & \text{if } x = \text{Cave} \\ \text{Fight Monster} & \text{if } x = \text{Monster} \\ \text{Find Treasure} & \text{if } x = \text{Treasure} \end{cases} \quad (1)$$

This equation metaphorically represents the choices players could make in Doug's game, showcasing the decision-making process that is fundamental in programming and game design.

High School Projects

As Doug progressed through high school, he took on more challenging projects. One notable endeavor was a program that simulated a simple physics engine, allowing users to visualize the motion of objects under various conditions. This project not only required a solid understanding of physics principles but also demanded proficiency in algorithms and data structures.

The core of the physics simulation could be summarized by the following equations of motion:

$$s = ut + \frac{1}{2}at^2 \qquad (2)$$

$$v = u + at \qquad (3)$$

Where:

- s = displacement
- u = initial velocity
- v = final velocity
- a = acceleration
- t = time

Through this project, Doug learned how to implement iterative methods to update the position and velocity of objects in real-time, further deepening his understanding of computational thinking.

College Ventures

Upon entering college, Doug's programming skills were put to the test as he tackled more complex projects. One of his significant projects involved developing a simple database management system in C. This project was particularly ambitious, as it required him to implement various data structures such as linked lists and trees to efficiently store and retrieve information.

The basic operations of the database can be represented as follows:

$$\text{Insert}(x) \rightarrow \text{Node}(x) \qquad (4)$$

$$\text{Search}(key) \rightarrow \text{Node if found, else NULL} \qquad (5)$$

This experience not only solidified his understanding of databases but also sparked his interest in the open-source community, where he would later make significant contributions.

The Influence of Open Source

Inspired by the collaborative spirit of the open-source movement, Doug began to contribute to various projects while still in college. He participated in a project that aimed to create a web crawler, a tool that would automatically browse the web and index content. This project introduced him to the challenges of distributed systems and the importance of efficient algorithms in web technologies.

The crawler's fundamental operation can be described by the following pseudocode:

```
function crawl(url):
    if url not in visited:
        mark\index{mark} as visited
        content = fetch(url)
        for link in extract_links(content):
            crawl(link)
```

This recursive algorithm highlights the essence of web crawling, illustrating how early programming projects can lead to complex systems that form the backbone of modern internet technologies.

Reflections on Early Projects

Reflecting on these early programming projects, it becomes evident that they were not merely academic exercises but rather stepping stones that shaped Doug Cutting's approach to software development. Each project presented unique challenges that required innovative solutions, fostering a mindset that would later prove invaluable in his career.

The combination of creativity, analytical thinking, and a collaborative spirit that Doug cultivated during these formative years would ultimately lead to groundbreaking contributions in the field of data processing, particularly with the development of Hadoop. These early experiences were instrumental in establishing the foundation for a career defined by innovation and a commitment to open-source principles.

In conclusion, Doug Cutting's early programming projects were more than just code; they were the building blocks of a visionary's journey, setting the stage for his future achievements in the tech industry. As he moved forward, the lessons learned from these projects would echo throughout his career, influencing his approach to problem-solving and collaboration in the ever-evolving landscape of technology.

The Birth of an Innovator

The journey of Doug Cutting from a curious child to a groundbreaking innovator in the tech world is a tale woven with threads of passion, intellect, and an unyielding quest for solutions. Born in the vibrant era of the 1970s, Doug was surrounded by the burgeoning field of computer science, which would soon become the canvas for his innovative spirit.

Early Inspirations

Doug's early inspirations can be traced back to the whimsical world of science fiction and technology. Books such as *The Hitchhiker's Guide to the Galaxy* and the works of Isaac Asimov ignited his imagination, fostering a belief that technology could solve complex problems. This literary foundation was further enriched by his exposure to early computers, where he began to appreciate the intricacies of programming and the potential for innovation.

Problem-Solving Mindset

An essential quality that marked Doug's development as an innovator was his problem-solving mindset. From a young age, he was drawn to puzzles and challenges, often spending hours tinkering with electronics and coding small programs. This hands-on approach not only honed his technical skills but also instilled a deep understanding of the iterative nature of innovation.

$$Innovation = \frac{\text{Creativity} \times \text{Problem-Solving}}{\text{Persistence}} \qquad (6)$$

In this equation, creativity and problem-solving are multiplied, emphasizing the need for both elements to achieve true innovation. However, persistence, represented in the denominator, is crucial; without it, even the most creative ideas may falter.

The Role of Education

Education played a pivotal role in Doug's journey. His formal studies at Stanford University provided him with a robust foundation in computer science. Here, he was not only exposed to the theoretical underpinnings of algorithms and data structures but also to collaborative projects that fostered his ability to innovate within a team. The synergy of diverse ideas often led to breakthroughs that Doug would carry into his professional career.

CAREER BEGINNINGS

First Steps in Innovation

Doug's first steps into the world of innovation began with his work on early programming projects. One notable project was a search engine called *Nutch*, which he co-created in the early 2000s. Nutch was designed to index web content, and its development highlighted several challenges, including the need for efficient data storage and retrieval systems. Doug's innovative approach to these challenges laid the groundwork for future advancements.

The Catalyst for Hadoop

The birth of Hadoop can be traced back to the necessity for a scalable solution to handle massive datasets. As the internet expanded, so did the volume of data generated. Doug recognized that traditional data processing methods were insufficient for this new reality. His innovative spirit drove him to explore distributed computing, leading to the creation of Hadoop.

$$\text{Scalability} = \text{Data Volume} \times \text{Processing Speed} \qquad (7)$$

In this equation, scalability is directly proportional to both data volume and processing speed, underscoring the importance of innovative solutions that can handle increasing amounts of data efficiently.

Conclusion

In conclusion, the birth of Doug Cutting as an innovator was not a singular event but rather a culmination of influences, experiences, and a relentless pursuit of solutions. His journey reflects the essence of innovation: a blend of creativity, problem-solving, and the courage to tackle challenges head-on. As we delve deeper into his contributions to the tech world, it becomes evident that Doug's innovative spirit has not only shaped his career but has also paved the way for future generations of programmers and technologists.

Career Beginnings

First Job in the Tech Industry

Doug Cutting's journey into the tech industry began with a pivotal first job that would set the stage for his future innovations. After completing his education, Doug found himself at a crossroads, eager to apply his skills in a professional environment. His first role was at a small startup, where he was tasked with developing software solutions that addressed real-world problems. This opportunity allowed him to immerse himself in the fast-paced world of technology, where creativity and technical prowess were essential.

The Startup Environment

The startup environment is often characterized by its dynamic nature and the need for rapid problem-solving. Doug's first job was no exception. He joined a team that was focused on creating a search engine, a concept that was gaining traction in the early days of the internet. This role required him to wear multiple hats, from coding to collaborating with designers and product managers.

$$\text{Success} = \text{Innovation} + \text{Collaboration} \tag{8}$$

In this equation, Doug learned that innovation was not just about writing code; it was equally about collaborating with others to bring ideas to fruition. The synergy of teamwork was crucial in navigating the challenges that arose during the development process.

Technical Challenges

One of the significant challenges Doug faced in his first job was the need to optimize search algorithms for efficiency. At the time, many search engines struggled with speed and accuracy, leading to user frustration. Doug was tasked with improving the search functionality, which required a deep understanding of data structures and algorithms.

For instance, Doug utilized data structures such as `hash tables` and `binary trees` to enhance search efficiency. The choice of data structure directly influenced the performance of the search engine, as shown in the following equation:

$$\text{Time Complexity} = O(\log n) \quad \text{(for balanced trees)} \tag{9}$$

This equation illustrates how balanced trees can significantly reduce the time complexity of search operations compared to unstructured data storage methods.

Learning from Failure

Doug's early experiences were not without their setbacks. He encountered numerous failures, from bugs in the code to misaligned project goals. Each failure presented an opportunity for learning and growth. Doug adopted a mindset that embraced

CAREER BEGINNINGS 13

failure as a stepping stone to success. He often reflected on the lessons learned from these experiences, which shaped his approach to problem-solving in the future.

Networking and Collaboration

During his time at the startup, Doug recognized the importance of networking within the tech community. He attended local meetups and conferences, where he engaged with other programmers and industry leaders. These interactions not only expanded his knowledge but also opened doors to future collaborations.

One notable connection was with a fellow programmer who introduced him to the concept of open-source software. This idea resonated deeply with Doug, as it aligned with his belief in collaboration and community-driven development. The principles of open-source would later play a significant role in his career, particularly with the development of Hadoop.

Conclusion

Doug Cutting's first job in the tech industry was a formative experience that laid the groundwork for his future successes. The combination of technical challenges, collaborative efforts, and a willingness to learn from failures set him on a path toward innovation. This early exposure to the startup culture and the importance of networking would become instrumental as he navigated the evolving landscape of technology, ultimately leading to his groundbreaking work with Hadoop.

In summary, Doug's first job was not just a stepping stone but a crucible that forged his skills, values, and vision for the future of computing. The lessons he learned during this period would resonate throughout his career, influencing his approach to technology and collaboration in the years to come.

Early Ventures and Contributions

Doug Cutting's journey into the tech industry was marked by a series of early ventures that not only showcased his programming prowess but also highlighted his commitment to innovation and collaboration. These formative experiences laid the groundwork for his later successes, particularly in the realm of big data and open source software.

First Steps in the Tech Industry

After graduating from the University of California, Santa Cruz, Doug Cutting took his first steps into the tech industry at a small company called *Essex*

Corporation. Here, he was introduced to the challenges and intricacies of software development. His role involved working on various projects that required both creativity and technical skill. It was during this time that he became aware of the power of collaborative software development, which would later become a cornerstone of his career.

Contributions to the Apache Software Foundation

Doug's early ventures were significantly influenced by his involvement with the *Apache Software Foundation* (ASF). In the late 1990s, he began contributing to the Apache Lucene project, a high-performance, full-featured text search engine library. His contributions included enhancing the search capabilities and optimizing the performance of the engine. This experience not only honed his technical skills but also instilled in him a deep appreciation for open source principles.

The Apache Lucene project, which Doug co-founded, was pivotal in demonstrating the viability of open source software for commercial applications. The success of Lucene led to the development of numerous derivative projects, solidifying Doug's reputation as a thought leader in the open source community.

The Birth of Nutch

Building on the success of Lucene, Doug Cutting initiated another ambitious project: *Nutch*. Launched in 2002, Nutch was an open-source web crawler and search engine framework that leveraged the capabilities of Lucene. Doug's vision for Nutch was to create a scalable search engine that could index vast amounts of web data.

Nutch faced several challenges, including the need for efficient crawling algorithms and effective data storage solutions. Doug tackled these issues by implementing a modular architecture that allowed developers to plug in different components as needed. This flexibility was crucial in adapting to the rapidly changing landscape of the web.

The Nutch project not only showcased Doug's technical acumen but also emphasized the importance of community collaboration. By encouraging contributions from developers around the world, Doug fostered a vibrant ecosystem that enriched the project and expanded its capabilities.

The Open Source Ethos

Doug Cutting's early ventures were deeply rooted in the open source ethos, which values transparency, collaboration, and community-driven development. He believed that software should be accessible to everyone, and this belief guided his work on both Lucene and Nutch. The success of these projects demonstrated that open source software could compete with proprietary solutions, paving the way for a new era in software development.

In his early career, Doug also participated in various conferences and workshops, where he shared his insights on open source development and the importance of community engagement. His talks often emphasized the need for developers to collaborate and share knowledge, which resonated with many in the tech community.

Lessons Learned

Through his early ventures, Doug Cutting learned valuable lessons about the importance of perseverance and adaptability. The challenges he faced while developing Nutch and contributing to Lucene taught him the significance of iterative development and the need to embrace feedback from users and contributors.

One of the key problems Doug encountered was the scalability of search technologies. As the web grew exponentially, traditional search engines struggled to keep pace. Doug's experience with Nutch allowed him to explore innovative solutions, such as distributed computing and advanced indexing techniques, which would later inform his work on Hadoop.

Conclusion

Doug Cutting's early ventures and contributions laid the foundation for his future successes in the tech industry. His work on Lucene and Nutch not only showcased his technical skills but also highlighted his commitment to the open source community. These experiences shaped his understanding of collaboration, innovation, and the transformative power of technology, ultimately leading to the creation of Hadoop and revolutionizing the way we handle big data.

As we delve deeper into Doug's journey, it becomes clear that his early ventures were not merely stepping stones but rather integral components of a larger narrative that would redefine data processing and analytics in the years to come.

Exploring New Technologies

As Doug Cutting embarked on his journey in the tech industry, he quickly recognized that the landscape of computing was evolving at an unprecedented pace. The late 1990s and early 2000s marked a significant turning point in technology, characterized by the rise of the Internet, the proliferation of personal computing, and the growing importance of data. This subsection delves into Cutting's early explorations of new technologies that would shape his future contributions to the field.

The Emergence of Distributed Computing

One of the pivotal areas that Cutting explored was distributed computing. The need for systems that could efficiently process large volumes of data across multiple machines became apparent. Traditional computing models were often limited by the constraints of single-machine processing. As a result, Cutting began to investigate frameworks that allowed for the distribution of workloads across clusters of computers.

The theoretical foundation of distributed computing can be expressed through the concept of *MapReduce*, a programming model that simplifies the processing of large data sets. The MapReduce algorithm can be summarized in two main functions: the Map function, which processes input data and produces key-value pairs, and the Reduce function, which aggregates the results based on the keys. Mathematically, this can be represented as:

$$\text{Map} : (k_1, v_1) \to \{(k_2, v_2)\}$$

$$\text{Reduce} : (k_2, \{v_2\}) \to (k_3, v_3)$$

This model not only provided a way to handle large datasets but also introduced a paradigm shift in how programmers approached data processing tasks. Cutting's early experiments with distributed systems laid the groundwork for his later work on Hadoop.

Open Source Software Movement

Another significant influence on Cutting was the open source software movement, which encouraged collaboration and innovation through shared codebases. The philosophy behind open source is rooted in the belief that software should be freely accessible, allowing developers to modify and enhance it for their purposes. This movement resonated with Cutting, who saw the potential for community-driven development.

During this period, he became involved with various open source projects, contributing to the development of tools that would later become integral to his work. For example, his contributions to the Apache Lucene project provided him with insights into search technologies and indexing, which would become essential components of Hadoop.

Challenges in Adopting New Technologies

While exploring new technologies, Cutting faced several challenges. One of the primary obstacles was the integration of disparate systems and ensuring compatibility across various platforms. As organizations began to adopt more complex architectures, the need for seamless interoperability became critical.

The challenge of data silos, where information is trapped within isolated systems, also emerged as a significant problem. Organizations often struggled to harness the full potential of their data due to fragmentation. Cutting's exploration of distributed computing and open source solutions aimed to address these issues, promoting a more unified approach to data management.

Real-World Applications and Early Successes

Cutting's foray into new technologies was not just theoretical; it was also practical. He worked on several projects that demonstrated the real-world applicability of distributed computing and open source software. One notable example was his involvement in the Nutch project, an open source web search engine built on the principles of distributed computing.

Nutch utilized a modified version of the MapReduce paradigm to crawl the web and index content efficiently. This project highlighted the potential of using distributed systems for large-scale data processing and laid the groundwork for the development of Hadoop. The success of Nutch served as a testament to the viability of these emerging technologies and inspired further exploration.

Conclusion

In conclusion, Doug Cutting's exploration of new technologies during his early career was marked by a keen awareness of the evolving tech landscape. His investigations into distributed computing and the open source movement not only shaped his professional trajectory but also contributed to the broader technological advancements of the time. These experiences set the stage for his future innovations, including the creation of Hadoop, which would revolutionize the way organizations handle big data. As Cutting continued to embrace new technologies, he remained committed to fostering collaboration and driving innovation within the tech community.

Influence of Open Source Community

The open source community has played a pivotal role in shaping the career of Doug Cutting and the development of Hadoop. This subsection explores the multifaceted influence of open source principles, collaboration, and community engagement that have been instrumental in the evolution of technology and innovation.

The Open Source Philosophy

At the heart of the open source movement lies a philosophy that promotes transparency, collaboration, and shared knowledge. The ethos of open source is encapsulated in the phrase, "With enough eyeballs, all bugs are shallow," coined by Eric S. Raymond in his essay *The Cathedral and the Bazaar*. This principle suggests that the more people who can inspect and contribute to a codebase, the more likely it is that errors will be identified and resolved efficiently. Doug Cutting embraced this philosophy early in his career, recognizing its potential to accelerate innovation and foster a vibrant developer community.

Collaboration and Networking

Doug Cutting's journey in the tech industry was significantly influenced by his active participation in the open source community. Collaboration became a cornerstone of his work, allowing him to connect with like-minded developers and industry experts. The open source community provided a platform for Cutting to share ideas, seek feedback, and collaborate on projects that pushed the boundaries of technology.

For instance, while developing Hadoop, Cutting leveraged the collective expertise of the community to address challenges that arose during the project. The ability to tap into a diverse pool of talent and experience facilitated the rapid iteration and improvement of the Hadoop framework. This collaborative spirit is exemplified in the way contributors from various backgrounds came together to enhance Hadoop's functionality, scalability, and performance.

Community-Driven Development

One of the defining features of open source projects is the emphasis on community-driven development. This approach empowers users and developers to contribute to the codebase, report issues, and suggest enhancements. In the case of Hadoop, the community's involvement was crucial in identifying real-world use cases and addressing the specific needs of enterprises.

The Apache Software Foundation (ASF), which oversees the development of Hadoop, embodies the principles of open source governance. The ASF provides a structured environment where contributors can collaborate, maintain quality control, and ensure that the project remains aligned with the needs of its users. This governance model fosters an inclusive atmosphere where diverse voices are heard, leading to more robust and innovative solutions.

The Role of Documentation and Education

An essential aspect of the open source community is the emphasis on documentation and education. Doug Cutting recognized that for Hadoop to gain traction, it was imperative to provide comprehensive documentation that would enable new users to understand and utilize the framework effectively. This commitment to education not only facilitated adoption but also empowered users to contribute back to the project.

The availability of tutorials, guides, and forums created an ecosystem where users could learn from one another, share best practices, and troubleshoot issues collaboratively. This culture of knowledge sharing has been instrumental in fostering a sense of community ownership over Hadoop, as users feel invested in the project's success.

Challenges and Criticisms

While the open source community has been a driving force behind Hadoop's success, it has not been without its challenges. The decentralized nature of open source projects can sometimes lead to fragmentation, where multiple versions of a project exist without a clear path for integration. This issue can create confusion among users and hinder the overall progress of the project.

Moreover, the reliance on community contributions can result in varying levels of quality and commitment. While many contributors are passionate and dedicated, others may lack the time or expertise to deliver high-quality code. Doug Cutting and the Hadoop team faced the challenge of maintaining a cohesive vision for the project while navigating the complexities of community-driven development.

Success Stories and Impact

Despite these challenges, the influence of the open source community on Hadoop has yielded remarkable success stories. Organizations across various industries have adopted Hadoop to tackle their big data challenges, leading to innovative applications and solutions. For example, companies like Yahoo! and Facebook have leveraged Hadoop to process vast amounts of data, enabling them to gain valuable insights and drive business decisions.

The success of Hadoop has also inspired a new generation of open source projects, further cementing the importance of community collaboration in the tech industry. Projects like Apache Spark and Apache Flink have emerged, building on the principles established by Hadoop and showcasing the power of open source innovation.

Conclusion

In conclusion, the influence of the open source community on Doug Cutting's career and the development of Hadoop cannot be overstated. The collaborative spirit, community-driven development, and commitment to education have shaped Hadoop into a transformative force in the world of big data. As Cutting continues to explore new frontiers in data processing, the lessons learned from the open source community will undoubtedly guide his efforts and inspire future innovations.

The open source movement represents a paradigm shift in how technology is developed and shared, and Doug Cutting's journey exemplifies the profound impact that community engagement can have on shaping the future of computing. Through collaboration, knowledge sharing, and a shared vision for progress, the open source community continues to drive innovation and empower developers around the globe.

Collaboration and Networking

In the fast-paced world of technology, collaboration and networking are not just beneficial; they are essential for innovation and success. Doug Cutting, a visionary in the realm of big data, understood this principle early in his career. His journey through the tech industry is a testament to the power of building relationships and fostering teamwork.

The Importance of Collaboration

Collaboration in software development, particularly in open-source projects, is crucial for several reasons:

- **Diverse Perspectives:** Working with others brings together a variety of ideas and perspectives. This diversity can lead to more creative solutions and more robust software.

- **Shared Knowledge:** Collaboration allows for the sharing of expertise and knowledge. Developers can learn from each other, which accelerates personal and project growth.

- **Resource Optimization:** By working together, teams can pool resources, whether they are time, skills, or tools, leading to more efficient project completion.

Doug Cutting exemplified these principles through his early involvement in the open-source community. He recognized that the collective intelligence of a group could lead to breakthroughs that an individual might not achieve alone.

Networking: Building Connections

Networking is another critical aspect of Doug Cutting's career. Effective networking involves building and maintaining relationships that can provide support, insights, and opportunities. Doug's ability to network effectively can be illustrated through several key points:

- **Engagement with the Open Source Community:** Doug was an active participant in various open-source forums and conferences. This engagement allowed him to connect with like-minded individuals, share ideas, and collaborate on projects. For instance, his work on Apache Lucene and Nutch involved numerous contributors who brought their expertise to the table.

- **Mentorship and Guidance:** Throughout his career, Doug sought mentorship from experienced professionals in the tech industry. This guidance was instrumental in shaping his approach to problem-solving and innovation. He, in turn, has mentored many aspiring programmers, creating a cycle of knowledge transfer that benefits the entire community.

- **Industry Collaborations:** Doug's collaborations with various tech companies and institutions have been pivotal in advancing his projects. For example, the partnership between Yahoo! and Doug Cutting led to the development of Hadoop, which was initially created to meet Yahoo!'s need for a scalable data processing framework. This collaboration not only provided the necessary resources but also validated Hadoop's potential in the industry.

Challenges in Collaboration

Despite the benefits, collaboration is not without its challenges. Doug Cutting faced several obstacles in his collaborative efforts:

- **Communication Barriers:** Working with a diverse group of individuals can lead to misunderstandings. Doug had to develop effective communication strategies to ensure that all team members were aligned on project goals and expectations.

- **Conflict Resolution:** Differences in opinion are natural in collaborative environments. Doug learned to navigate conflicts by promoting open dialogue and focusing on common objectives, which helped maintain a positive working atmosphere.

- **Balancing Contributions:** In collaborative projects, it can be challenging to ensure that all contributors feel valued and that their input is recognized. Doug made it a priority to acknowledge the efforts of his collaborators, fostering a culture of respect and appreciation.

Examples of Successful Collaboration

One of the most notable examples of Doug Cutting's collaborative success is the development of Hadoop. The project began as a solution to a specific problem at Yahoo! but quickly evolved into a community-driven initiative. The collaborative nature of Hadoop's development is evident in its architecture, which was designed to be extensible and adaptable to various use cases.

$$H = \{N_1, N_2, N_3, \ldots, N_n\} \tag{10}$$

where H represents Hadoop and N_i represents the nodes in the distributed system. Each node can be developed and maintained by different contributors, showcasing the essence of collaboration in its architecture.

Another example is the Apache Software Foundation (ASF), where Doug Cutting played a significant role. The ASF provides a collaborative environment for developers to contribute to open-source projects. Doug's active participation in the ASF allowed him to connect with other innovators and expand his influence in the open-source community.

Conclusion

In conclusion, Doug Cutting's career highlights the significance of collaboration and networking in the tech industry. His ability to build relationships, engage with the open-source community, and navigate the challenges of teamwork has been instrumental in his success and the evolution of Hadoop. As technology continues to advance, the importance of collaboration will only grow, making Doug's experiences a valuable lesson for future generations of programmers.

The Rise of Hadoop

Inception of Hadoop

The Need for a Better Solution

In the early 2000s, the explosion of data generated by businesses, social media, and the internet posed a significant challenge for traditional data processing systems. As organizations began to recognize the value of data analytics, they faced limitations with existing database technologies, which were primarily designed for structured data and relational models. The need for a better solution to manage and process vast amounts of unstructured and semi-structured data became increasingly evident.

The Data Deluge

The term "data deluge" refers to the overwhelming amount of data generated every day. According to a report by IDC, the global datasphere was expected to reach 175 zettabytes by 2025, a staggering increase from 33 zettabytes in 2018. This rapid growth was driven by various factors, including:

- The proliferation of Internet of Things (IoT) devices, which continuously collect and transmit data.

- The rise of social media platforms, where users generate vast amounts of content.

- Increased digital transactions in e-commerce and online services.

The traditional databases struggled to keep pace with this deluge, as they were not designed to handle the volume, variety, and velocity of data that organizations were encountering.

Limitations of Traditional Data Processing

Traditional data processing systems, such as relational databases, exhibited several limitations:

1. **Scalability:** As data volumes grew, scaling traditional databases often required expensive hardware upgrades or complex sharding techniques. This was not only costly but also time-consuming, leading to potential downtime.

2. **Data Variety:** Traditional databases excelled in managing structured data but faltered with unstructured or semi-structured data, such as text, images, and videos. This limitation restricted organizations from fully leveraging their data assets.

3. **Processing Speed:** The need for real-time analytics became crucial in various industries. Traditional systems often struggled to provide timely insights, resulting in missed opportunities for businesses.

4. **Cost:** The licensing fees for traditional database systems, combined with the costs of hardware and maintenance, made them prohibitively expensive for many organizations, especially startups and small businesses.

These limitations highlighted a pressing need for a new approach to data processing, one that could effectively manage large-scale data while being cost-efficient and flexible.

Emergence of Distributed Computing

The concept of distributed computing emerged as a potential solution to the challenges posed by the data deluge. Distributed computing involves spreading data processing tasks across multiple machines, allowing for parallel processing and improved efficiency. This approach offered several advantages:

- **Horizontal Scalability:** Organizations could add more machines to their network to handle increased workloads, rather than relying on a single powerful server.

- **Fault Tolerance:** By distributing data across multiple nodes, systems could be designed to continue functioning even if one or more nodes failed.

- **Cost-Effectiveness:** Utilizing commodity hardware for distributed systems reduced costs significantly compared to traditional high-end servers.

INCEPTION OF HADOOP

The need for a robust, scalable, and cost-effective solution to manage the complexities of big data led to the birth of Hadoop, a framework that harnessed the power of distributed computing to address these challenges.

Conclusion

In summary, the demand for a better solution to manage and process the ever-growing volumes of data was clear. Traditional systems were unable to cope with the scale, variety, and speed required by modern enterprises. The emergence of distributed computing provided a promising avenue for innovation, paving the way for the development of Hadoop. Doug Cutting, recognizing this need, embarked on a journey to create a framework that would revolutionize the way organizations handled big data, setting the stage for a new era in data processing.

Inspiration and Research

The inception of Hadoop can be traced back to a confluence of inspirations and rigorous research that addressed the burgeoning challenges of data processing in the early 2000s. Doug Cutting, motivated by the increasing need for scalable and efficient data storage solutions, found himself at the intersection of innovation and necessity.

One of the primary inspirations for Hadoop came from Google's groundbreaking paper titled "MapReduce: Simplified Data Processing on Large Clusters" [?]. This seminal work introduced a programming model and an associated implementation for processing and generating large data sets with a parallel, distributed algorithm on a cluster. The MapReduce framework allows for the processing of vast amounts of data by breaking down tasks into smaller, manageable chunks. The model comprises two main functions: *Map* and *Reduce*.

The *Map* function processes input data into key-value pairs, while the *Reduce* function aggregates these pairs to produce the final output. Mathematically, this can be represented as:

$$\text{Map}(k_1, v_1) \rightarrow \{(k_2, v_2)\}$$

$$\text{Reduce}(k_2, \{v_2\}) \rightarrow v_3$$

This approach not only simplified the programming model for data processing but also highlighted the need for fault tolerance and scalability in distributed systems.

In addition to the MapReduce framework, Doug was influenced by the Google File System (GFS) paper [?], which presented a scalable distributed file system designed to accommodate large amounts of data across numerous machines. GFS's architecture allowed for high throughput access to application data, making it an essential reference for developing a robust storage solution to support Hadoop's processing capabilities. The design principles of GFS emphasized the importance of redundancy and data integrity, which became cornerstones of Hadoop's architecture.

The combination of these two revolutionary concepts—MapReduce for processing and GFS for storage—sparked the initial research phase for Hadoop. Doug recognized that to build an effective solution, he needed to address several critical problems that the industry faced:

1. **Scalability**: As data volumes grew exponentially, traditional databases struggled to keep up. Hadoop's architecture was designed to scale horizontally by adding more machines to the cluster, allowing organizations to manage larger datasets effectively.

2. **Fault Tolerance**: In distributed systems, hardware failures are inevitable. Hadoop's design incorporated data replication across multiple nodes, ensuring that even if one node failed, the data remained accessible. This principle was inspired by GFS's approach to data redundancy.

3. **Cost Efficiency**: The need for affordable data processing solutions was paramount. Hadoop leveraged commodity hardware rather than relying on expensive, high-end servers, making it accessible to a broader range of organizations.

4. **Flexibility**: The ability to handle various data types—from structured to unstructured—was crucial. Hadoop's schema-on-read approach allowed data to be stored without a predefined schema, enabling users to define the structure as they processed the data.

During the research phase, Doug and his team conducted numerous experiments to validate their ideas. They built prototypes that demonstrated the viability of the MapReduce model on clusters of commodity hardware. These experiments yielded promising results, showcasing Hadoop's ability to process large datasets efficiently.

One notable example was the implementation of a web crawler using the MapReduce paradigm. The team was able to index vast amounts of web data, demonstrating Hadoop's capacity to handle real-world data processing challenges. This practical application underscored the framework's potential and inspired further development.

Additionally, Doug engaged with the open-source community, seeking feedback and collaboration. The vibrant ecosystem of developers and researchers contributed to refining Hadoop's architecture and expanding its capabilities. This collaborative spirit was instrumental in shaping Hadoop into a robust platform that addressed the needs of various industries.

In conclusion, the inspiration and research behind Hadoop were rooted in addressing the pressing challenges of data processing in a rapidly evolving digital landscape. By synthesizing the principles of MapReduce and GFS, Doug Cutting laid the groundwork for a transformative framework that would revolutionize the way organizations handle big data. The journey from inspiration to implementation was marked by a commitment to innovation, collaboration, and an unwavering focus on solving real-world problems.

Building the Initial Framework

The journey of creating the initial framework for Hadoop was not merely a technical endeavor; it was a confluence of vision, necessity, and the collaborative spirit of the open-source community. At its core, Hadoop was designed to address the burgeoning challenges posed by the explosion of data in the early 2000s, particularly in the realms of storage and processing. This subsection delves into the theoretical underpinnings, the problems encountered, and the practical steps taken to build the foundation of what would become a revolutionary technology.

Theoretical Foundations

The initial framework of Hadoop was heavily influenced by the Google File System (GFS) and the MapReduce programming model, both of which were introduced in seminal papers by Google researchers. GFS provided a scalable architecture for distributed storage, while MapReduce offered a paradigm for processing vast amounts of data in parallel across clusters of machines.

The theoretical basis for Hadoop can be summarized as follows:

$$\text{Data} = \text{Storage} + \text{Processing} \tag{11}$$

This equation encapsulates the dual challenge that Hadoop sought to solve: how to efficiently store and process data across distributed systems. The necessity for a framework that could handle both aspects was paramount, especially as organizations began to grapple with the implications of big data.

Identifying the Problems

As Doug Cutting and his team embarked on building Hadoop, they faced several critical challenges:

1. **Scalability**: Traditional databases struggled to scale horizontally. The need for a system that could easily add nodes to accommodate growing data volumes was essential.

2. **Fault Tolerance**: In a distributed environment, the likelihood of hardware failures increases. A robust fault tolerance mechanism was necessary to ensure data integrity and availability.

3. **Data Variety**: The types of data being generated were diverse, ranging from structured to unstructured. The framework had to be adaptable to various data formats.

4. **Cost Efficiency**: Given the constraints of many organizations, particularly startups, Hadoop had to be built on commodity hardware to keep costs manageable.

5. **Ease of Use**: While powerful, the system had to be accessible to developers and data scientists who may not have a deep understanding of distributed computing.

Development Process

The initial development of Hadoop began with the adaptation of the MapReduce model. Doug Cutting, inspired by the need for a scalable solution, started by implementing the following key components:

- **Hadoop Distributed File System (HDFS)**: The backbone of Hadoop, HDFS was designed to store large files across multiple machines. It divides files into blocks (default size 128 MB) and replicates them across the cluster to ensure fault tolerance. The replication factor is typically set to three, meaning each block is stored on three different nodes.

- **MapReduce Engine**: This engine facilitated the processing of data in parallel. The process is divided into two main functions:
    - Map Function: This takes a set of data and converts it into key-value pairs. For example, if processing a log file, the map function might output the number of occurrences of each word:

$$\text{map}(k_1, v_1) \rightarrow \{(k_2, v_2)\} \tag{12}$$

INCEPTION OF HADOOP

- **Reduce Function**: This aggregates the output from the map function, combining values based on their keys:

$$\text{reduce}(k_2, \{v_2\}) \rightarrow (k_2, v_3) \qquad (13)$$

- **Job Tracker and Task Tracker**: The job tracker manages the scheduling of tasks across the cluster, while task trackers run the tasks on individual nodes, reporting back to the job tracker.

Early Prototyping and Testing

The first prototype of Hadoop was built in 2005, and it was crucial to test the framework in real-world scenarios. Doug Cutting and his team utilized a small cluster of computers to simulate larger data processing tasks. One of the first significant tests involved processing a dataset from the Nutch project, which was an open-source web crawler.

This initial testing phase revealed several performance bottlenecks, particularly in the areas of network I/O and data locality. To address these issues, the team iterated on the design, optimizing the way data was read and written to HDFS, and ensuring that computation was performed as close to the data as possible, thus minimizing data transfer across the network.

Community Engagement and Open Source Philosophy

A pivotal aspect of building Hadoop's initial framework was the commitment to open-source principles. Doug Cutting recognized that engaging with the developer community would not only enhance the framework but also foster innovation. By releasing Hadoop as an open-source project under the Apache Software Foundation, Cutting invited contributions from developers worldwide, leading to rapid enhancements and a growing ecosystem.

This collaborative approach allowed for diverse perspectives and expertise to converge, resulting in a more robust and versatile framework. The community's feedback was invaluable, helping to identify bugs, suggest features, and improve documentation.

Conclusion

The building of Hadoop's initial framework was a complex, multifaceted process that combined theoretical knowledge, practical problem-solving, and community collaboration. By addressing the challenges of scalability, fault tolerance, and data variety, Doug Cutting laid the groundwork for a technology that would revolutionize data processing. The iterative development process, coupled with the open-source philosophy, not only led to a successful framework but also established Hadoop as a cornerstone of big data technologies, paving the way for future innovations.

In summary, the initial framework of Hadoop was a testament to the power of vision, collaboration, and the relentless pursuit of solutions to pressing data challenges. As we move forward in this biography, we will explore how Hadoop evolved and its lasting impact on the tech industry.

Hadoop's Unique Features

Hadoop, an open-source framework designed for distributed storage and processing of large datasets, is characterized by several unique features that set it apart from traditional data processing systems. Understanding these features is crucial for appreciating Hadoop's impact on the big data landscape.

1. Scalability

One of Hadoop's standout features is its scalability. Hadoop can efficiently process petabytes of data by scaling horizontally, which means that additional nodes can be added to the cluster without requiring significant changes to the existing infrastructure. This is in stark contrast to traditional systems that often require vertical scaling (upgrading existing hardware), which can be both costly and time-consuming.

The scalability of Hadoop is primarily facilitated by its distributed file system, HDFS (Hadoop Distributed File System), which allows data to be stored across multiple machines. The scalability can be mathematically expressed as:

$$\text{Total Storage Capacity} = N \times S$$

where N is the number of nodes in the cluster and S is the storage capacity of each node. This equation highlights how the total storage capacity increases linearly with the addition of more nodes.

2. Fault Tolerance

Hadoop is designed with fault tolerance in mind. In a distributed environment, hardware failures are inevitable, but Hadoop's architecture ensures that the system continues to function even when individual nodes fail. This is achieved through data

INCEPTION OF HADOOP

replication. Each data block in HDFS is replicated across multiple nodes (by default, three copies), allowing the system to recover from failures seamlessly.

For instance, if a node storing a block of data goes down, Hadoop automatically redirects requests to another node that holds a replica of the same block. This replication strategy can be represented as:

$$\text{Number of Replicas} = R$$

where R is the replication factor. The robustness of this feature is crucial for maintaining data integrity and availability, especially in critical applications.

3. Data Locality

Hadoop's ability to move computation closer to where the data resides is another unique feature. This concept, known as data locality, minimizes network congestion and reduces the time required for data processing. Instead of transferring large datasets across the network to a centralized processing unit, Hadoop allows processing tasks to run on the same nodes that store the data.

This is particularly beneficial in large-scale data processing scenarios, where transferring massive amounts of data can be a bottleneck. The efficiency of data locality can be illustrated with the following example:

- Suppose a dataset of 1 TB is distributed across 10 nodes in a Hadoop cluster.

- If a MapReduce job processes this data, it can run simultaneously on each node, reducing the need to transfer data over the network.

- As a result, the time taken to complete the job is significantly reduced compared to traditional systems where data is moved to a single processing node.

4. Flexibility

Hadoop's schema-on-read capability offers flexibility that is unparalleled in conventional databases. In traditional relational databases, data must conform to a predefined schema before it can be stored. In contrast, Hadoop allows you to store data in its raw form, regardless of its structure. This means that you can ingest structured, semi-structured, and unstructured data without prior transformation.

For example, consider a scenario where a company collects user interaction data from various sources, including social media, web logs, and transactional databases. With Hadoop, the company can store all this data in its original format and apply different processing techniques later, depending on the analysis requirements. This flexibility is particularly advantageous in dynamic environments where data types and structures may evolve over time.

5. Cost-Effectiveness

Hadoop is designed to run on commodity hardware, which significantly reduces the cost of data storage and processing. Organizations can build Hadoop clusters using inexpensive machines rather than investing in high-end servers. This cost-effectiveness democratizes access to big data technologies, enabling small and medium-sized enterprises (SMEs) to leverage data analytics without incurring prohibitive expenses.

$$\text{Total Cost} = \sum_{i=1}^{N} C_i \qquad (14)$$

where C_i represents the cost of each node in the cluster. As the costs of commodity hardware continue to decrease, the overall cost of deploying a Hadoop cluster becomes increasingly attractive.

6. Strong Community Support

Finally, one of Hadoop's unique features is its strong community support. Being an open-source project, Hadoop benefits from contributions from developers worldwide. This collaborative environment fosters innovation and rapid development of new features, tools, and integrations. The Apache Software Foundation oversees Hadoop's development, ensuring a structured governance model and continuous improvement.

In conclusion, Hadoop's unique features—scalability, fault tolerance, data locality, flexibility, cost-effectiveness, and strong community support—have established it as a cornerstone technology in the big data ecosystem. These characteristics not only address the challenges of processing large datasets but also empower organizations to extract valuable insights from their data in a cost-efficient and reliable manner.

Early Adoption and Recognition

The journey of Hadoop from a nascent idea to a revolutionary framework in the realm of big data processing is a story marked by early adoption and significant recognition. The inception of Hadoop was not merely a technical endeavor; it was

INCEPTION OF HADOOP

a response to the burgeoning need for scalable data processing solutions in an increasingly data-driven world. As organizations began to recognize the limitations of traditional data processing systems, Hadoop emerged as a beacon of innovation.

The Initial User Base

In the early stages, Hadoop attracted a diverse group of early adopters, ranging from startups to large enterprises. These organizations were primarily drawn to Hadoop's ability to handle vast amounts of unstructured data, which was becoming more prevalent with the rise of the internet and social media. For instance, companies like Yahoo! were among the first to implement Hadoop in their data centers. Yahoo! utilized Hadoop to process and analyze petabytes of data generated from their search engine and other services. This early adoption not only validated Hadoop's capabilities but also provided critical feedback that shaped its development.

Community and Ecosystem Growth

The recognition of Hadoop's potential was further amplified by the open-source community, which played a pivotal role in its evolution. As developers and data scientists began to experiment with Hadoop, they shared their experiences, challenges, and solutions through forums and conferences. This collaborative environment fostered a rich ecosystem of tools and frameworks that complemented Hadoop, such as Apache Hive for data warehousing and Apache Pig for data flow scripting. The collective efforts of the community not only enhanced Hadoop's functionality but also expanded its user base.

Case Studies of Early Success

Several case studies exemplify Hadoop's early recognition and adoption:

1. **Facebook**: In 2007, Facebook adopted Hadoop to manage its rapidly growing data. The social media giant leveraged Hadoop to analyze user interactions and improve its advertising algorithms. This strategic use of Hadoop allowed Facebook to gain insights into user behavior, driving engagement and revenue.

2. **LinkedIn**: Similarly, LinkedIn utilized Hadoop to power its recommendation systems and analyze user connections. By processing vast amounts of data, LinkedIn was able to enhance user experience and provide personalized content, which significantly contributed to its growth.

3. **Netflix**: The streaming service recognized the potential of Hadoop in optimizing its content delivery and recommendation engines. By analyzing viewing patterns and preferences, Netflix was able to tailor its offerings to individual users, thereby increasing customer satisfaction and retention.

Recognition and Awards

As Hadoop gained traction, it garnered recognition from various industry bodies and publications. In 2011, the Apache Software Foundation awarded Hadoop the status of a Top-Level Project, a testament to its maturity and the strong community support behind it. This recognition not only solidified Hadoop's position in the tech landscape but also attracted further investment and development.

Moreover, Hadoop's impact on the industry was highlighted in numerous reports and studies. Gartner, a leading research and advisory company, included Hadoop in its "Hype Cycle for Big Data" reports, marking it as a transformative technology with the potential to revolutionize data processing. Such endorsements from reputable organizations further fueled Hadoop's adoption across various sectors, including finance, healthcare, and retail.

Challenges in Early Adoption

Despite its successes, early adopters faced several challenges when implementing Hadoop. Organizations often struggled with the complexity of setting up and managing Hadoop clusters. The learning curve associated with Hadoop's ecosystem tools, such as HDFS (Hadoop Distributed File System) and MapReduce, posed significant hurdles. Additionally, concerns about data security and governance emerged as critical issues, particularly for industries handling sensitive information.

To address these challenges, early adopters engaged in community forums and sought guidance from experienced users, fostering a culture of knowledge sharing. Over time, these efforts led to the development of best practices and tools that eased the adoption process, paving the way for Hadoop's widespread use.

Conclusion

In conclusion, the early adoption and recognition of Hadoop were driven by its innovative approach to data processing and the collaborative efforts of the open-source community. As organizations began to harness the power of Hadoop, they unlocked new possibilities for data analysis and decision-making. The success stories of early adopters not only validated Hadoop's capabilities but also laid the groundwork for its evolution into a cornerstone of big data technology. As we continue to explore the journey of Doug Cutting and Hadoop, it is essential to recognize the significance of these early milestones in shaping the future of data processing.

Hadoop's Impact on Big Data

Revolutionizing Data Storage and Processing

The advent of Hadoop marked a pivotal moment in the evolution of data storage and processing. Prior to its introduction, the conventional methods for handling large volumes of data were often inadequate, leading to inefficiencies and limitations that stifled innovation. With the exponential growth of data generated by businesses, social media, and IoT devices, the need for a robust solution became increasingly apparent.

The Challenge of Traditional Data Management

Traditional relational database management systems (RDBMS) were designed for structured data and were limited in their ability to scale horizontally. As data volumes grew, these systems struggled to maintain performance, leading to several key challenges:

- **Scalability:** RDBMS typically scale vertically, meaning that to handle more data, organizations had to invest in more powerful hardware. This approach is not only costly but also presents a single point of failure.

- **Cost:** The infrastructure required to manage large datasets using traditional databases was prohibitively expensive, especially for startups and small businesses.

- **Flexibility:** Traditional databases require a predefined schema, which limits the ability to adapt to new data types and structures. This rigidity can hinder innovation and responsiveness to market changes.

- **Performance:** As data volumes increased, query performance degraded, leading to longer wait times for insights and decision-making.

Hadoop's Innovative Approach

Hadoop introduced a paradigm shift in how organizations approached data storage and processing. Its core architecture is based on two primary components: the Hadoop Distributed File System (HDFS) and the MapReduce programming model.

Hadoop Distributed File System (HDFS) HDFS is designed to store vast amounts of data across a distributed network of machines. Key features include:

- **Data Replication:** HDFS automatically replicates data across multiple nodes, ensuring fault tolerance and high availability. By default, each data block is replicated three times, allowing the system to withstand node failures without data loss.

- **Horizontal Scalability:** Organizations can add more commodity hardware to the cluster to increase storage capacity and processing power without significant investment in specialized equipment.

- **Support for Various Data Types:** HDFS can store unstructured, semi-structured, and structured data, allowing organizations to work with a wide variety of data sources without the need for a predefined schema.

MapReduce Programming Model MapReduce is a programming model that enables the processing of large datasets in parallel across a Hadoop cluster. It consists of two main functions: the Map function and the Reduce function.

$$\text{Map}(key, value) \rightarrow list(key, value) \qquad (15)$$

The Map function processes input data and produces a set of intermediate key-value pairs. For example, in a word count application, the input might be a text file, and the output would be a list of words and their corresponding counts.

$$\text{Reduce}(key, list(values)) \rightarrow list(key, value) \qquad (16)$$

The Reduce function takes the intermediate key-value pairs produced by the Map function and aggregates them to produce the final output. Continuing with the word count example, the Reduce function would sum the counts for each unique word.

Real-World Applications and Success Stories

Hadoop's revolutionary approach to data storage and processing has led to its adoption across various industries, enabling organizations to derive insights from massive datasets. Some notable examples include:

- **Yahoo!** was one of the early adopters of Hadoop, using it to analyze web logs and improve their advertising targeting and user experience. By leveraging Hadoop, Yahoo! could process terabytes of data quickly and efficiently, leading to better decision-making and increased revenue.

- **Facebook** utilizes Hadoop to analyze user interactions and preferences, allowing them to optimize their algorithms for content delivery. With billions of daily interactions, Hadoop's ability to scale horizontally has been crucial in managing and processing this data.

- **Netflix** employs Hadoop for its recommendation engine, analyzing vast amounts of viewing data to suggest content to users. The ability to process diverse data types, from viewing habits to user ratings, has enhanced Netflix's ability to personalize the user experience.

Conclusion

In summary, Hadoop has revolutionized data storage and processing by addressing the challenges posed by traditional systems. Its innovative architecture, characterized by HDFS and the MapReduce programming model, has enabled organizations to scale efficiently, handle diverse data types, and derive valuable insights from large datasets. As businesses continue to navigate the complexities of big data, Hadoop remains a cornerstone technology, empowering them to harness the full potential of their data.

Solving the Scalability Problem

In the realm of big data, scalability is a critical factor that determines the effectiveness of data processing frameworks. As organizations accumulate vast amounts of data, the ability to efficiently scale systems to handle this growth becomes paramount. Hadoop, designed with scalability in mind, addresses these challenges through its architecture and operational methodologies.

Understanding Scalability

Scalability refers to the capability of a system to increase its capacity and performance as the workload grows. In the context of Hadoop, scalability can be categorized into two types:

- **Vertical Scalability (Scaling Up):** This involves adding more resources (CPU, RAM) to a single machine. While this can improve performance, it has limitations due to hardware constraints and cost.

- **Horizontal Scalability (Scaling Out):** This entails adding more machines to a cluster. Hadoop excels in this area, allowing organizations to expand their data processing capabilities by simply adding more nodes to the cluster.

Hadoop's Architecture for Scalability

Hadoop's architecture is inherently designed for horizontal scalability. The core components that facilitate this include:

- **Hadoop Distributed File System (HDFS):** HDFS splits files into large blocks (default is 128 MB) and distributes them across multiple nodes in a cluster. This distribution allows for parallel processing and efficient data retrieval.

- **MapReduce Framework:** This programming model enables the processing of large datasets in parallel across the Hadoop cluster. The Map phase processes data in parallel, while the Reduce phase aggregates the results. The ability to distribute tasks across multiple nodes is crucial for scalability.

- **YARN (Yet Another Resource Negotiator):** Introduced in Hadoop 2.0, YARN allows multiple data processing engines to run and share resources dynamically. It separates resource management from data processing, enabling better resource utilization and scalability.

Challenges in Scalability

Despite its strengths, Hadoop faces several challenges in scalability:

- **Data Locality:** As data is distributed across nodes, ensuring that processing occurs close to where data is stored is essential for performance. Hadoop tackles this by scheduling tasks on nodes that have the required data blocks, reducing data transfer times.

- **Network Bottlenecks:** As the number of nodes increases, so does the complexity of network communication. Hadoop's design mitigates this by using a master-slave architecture, where the NameNode manages metadata and DataNodes handle storage. This reduces the load on any single node.
- **Fault Tolerance:** In a scalable system, the likelihood of node failures increases. Hadoop's replication strategy, where data blocks are replicated across multiple nodes (default is three copies), ensures that data remains accessible even if some nodes fail.

Real-World Examples

Several organizations have successfully leveraged Hadoop's scalability to address their big data challenges:

- **Facebook:** With over 2.8 billion monthly active users, Facebook generates immense amounts of data. By utilizing Hadoop, Facebook can efficiently process and analyze user interactions, advertisements, and content, scaling its infrastructure to accommodate growth without sacrificing performance.
- **Yahoo!:** One of the early adopters of Hadoop, Yahoo! operates one of the largest Hadoop clusters in the world. By scaling horizontally, Yahoo! has been able to manage and analyze petabytes of data, improving its search capabilities and ad targeting strategies.
- **Netflix:** The streaming giant uses Hadoop to process and analyze viewing patterns, user preferences, and content recommendations. Its ability to scale with demand allows Netflix to provide a seamless user experience even during peak times.

Conclusion

Hadoop's ability to solve the scalability problem is one of its defining features. By embracing a distributed architecture and focusing on horizontal scalability, it enables organizations to handle growing datasets efficiently. As data continues to expand exponentially, Hadoop remains at the forefront of big data processing, providing the necessary tools and frameworks to scale operations effectively.

In summary, Hadoop's design philosophy and architecture not only address the scalability challenges but also empower organizations to harness the full potential of their data, paving the way for innovation and insights in an increasingly data-driven world.

Use Cases and Success Stories

Hadoop's emergence as a powerful framework for big data processing has led to numerous successful implementations across various industries. Its ability to handle vast amounts of data, coupled with its scalability and flexibility, has made it a go-to solution for organizations looking to harness the power of data analytics. In this section, we explore some notable use cases and success stories that highlight Hadoop's transformative impact on businesses and sectors.

1. Retail: Enhancing Customer Experience

One of the most compelling use cases of Hadoop is in the retail sector, where companies leverage its capabilities to enhance customer experience and optimize operations. For instance, a leading e-commerce giant utilized Hadoop to analyze customer behavior patterns from millions of transactions. By processing this data, they were able to implement personalized marketing strategies, leading to a significant increase in conversion rates.

The analysis involved the following steps:

$$\text{Customer Segmentation} = f(\text{Purchase History, Browsing Behavior, Demographics}) \tag{17}$$

This function allowed the retailer to categorize customers into distinct segments, enabling targeted promotions and personalized recommendations. As a result, they reported a 30% increase in sales attributed to these tailored marketing efforts.

2. Healthcare: Improving Patient Outcomes

In the healthcare industry, Hadoop has been instrumental in improving patient outcomes through advanced analytics. A prominent hospital network adopted Hadoop to integrate and analyze data from various sources, including electronic health records (EHR), lab results, and patient feedback. This comprehensive data analysis facilitated predictive modeling to identify patients at risk of readmission.

The predictive model was developed using the following logistic regression equation:

$$P(\text{Readmission}) = \frac{1}{1 + e^{-(\beta_0 + \beta_1 \times \text{Age} + \beta_2 \times \text{Comorbidities} + \ldots)}} \tag{18}$$

By identifying high-risk patients, the hospital implemented targeted interventions, resulting in a 20% reduction in readmission rates and improved patient satisfaction scores.

3. Finance: Fraud Detection

The finance sector has also seen significant benefits from Hadoop's capabilities, particularly in fraud detection. A major credit card company employed Hadoop to analyze transaction data in real-time, enabling them to identify fraudulent activities quickly. By utilizing machine learning algorithms on their Hadoop cluster, they developed a model that could flag suspicious transactions based on various parameters.

The fraud detection model utilized features such as:

$$\text{Suspicious Score} = w_1 \times \text{Transaction Amount} + w_2 \times \text{Location Variance} + w_3 \times \text{Time of Tra} \tag{19}$$

Where w_1, w_2, and w_3 are weights determined through training on historical data. This proactive approach led to a 50% reduction in fraudulent transactions, saving the company millions of dollars annually.

4. Telecommunications: Network Optimization

Telecommunications companies have leveraged Hadoop for network optimization and customer experience enhancement. One notable case involved a telecom provider that used Hadoop to analyze call data records (CDRs) to identify patterns of network congestion. By processing terabytes of data, they were able to pinpoint specific areas where upgrades were needed.

The optimization process included:

$$\text{Network Efficiency} = \frac{\text{Successful Calls}}{\text{Total Calls Attempted}} \tag{20}$$

By improving network efficiency, the company not only enhanced customer satisfaction but also reduced operational costs associated with network maintenance and upgrades.

5. Education: Data-Driven Decision Making

Educational institutions have also embraced Hadoop to drive data-informed decision-making. A large university implemented Hadoop to analyze student performance data, attendance records, and engagement metrics. This analysis aimed to identify at-risk students and provide timely interventions.

The intervention strategy was based on a predictive model:

$$\text{At-Risk Probability} = f(\text{Attendance Rate}, \text{Grades}, \text{Participation}) \quad (21)$$

The university reported a 15% increase in student retention rates as a direct result of targeted support initiatives based on the insights gained from their Hadoop-driven analysis.

Conclusion

These examples illustrate how Hadoop's capabilities extend far beyond simple data storage; it empowers organizations to extract valuable insights from their data, driving innovation and efficiency across various sectors. As industries continue to evolve and generate vast amounts of data, the role of Hadoop in facilitating data-driven decision-making will only become more critical, solidifying its position as a cornerstone of big data analytics.

The Growing Hadoop Ecosystem

The Hadoop ecosystem has blossomed into a vibrant and diverse collection of tools and technologies that complement and enhance its core framework. This growth has been driven by the increasing demand for big data processing and analytics, as well as the collaborative spirit of the open-source community. In this section, we will explore the components of the Hadoop ecosystem, the problems they address, and real-world examples that illustrate their effectiveness.

Core Components of the Hadoop Ecosystem

At the heart of the Hadoop ecosystem are several key components that work together to provide a comprehensive solution for big data management. These components include:

- **Hadoop Distributed File System (HDFS)**: HDFS is the storage layer of Hadoop, designed to store vast amounts of data across a distributed network of machines. It achieves fault tolerance through data replication, ensuring that data is safe even in the event of hardware failures. The fundamental equation governing HDFS's replication strategy can be expressed as:

$$R = \frac{N}{D}$$

where R is the replication factor, N is the total number of data blocks, and D is the number of data nodes. A common replication factor is 3, meaning each block is stored on three different nodes.

- **MapReduce:** This programming model allows for the processing of large data sets in parallel across a Hadoop cluster. It consists of two phases: the Map phase, where data is processed and transformed into key-value pairs, and the Reduce phase, where these pairs are aggregated. The efficiency of MapReduce can be represented by the equation:

$$T = O(\frac{N}{P}) + O(M)$$

where T is the total time taken, N is the size of the input data, P is the number of parallel processes, and M is the time taken for the final aggregation.

- **YARN (Yet Another Resource Negotiator):** YARN is the resource management layer of Hadoop, responsible for job scheduling and cluster resource management. It allows multiple data processing engines to run on a single Hadoop cluster, enhancing resource utilization.

- **Hive:** Hive is a data warehousing tool built on top of Hadoop that allows for querying and managing large datasets using a SQL-like language called HiveQL. It abstracts the complexity of MapReduce, making it easier for analysts to interact with big data.

- **Pig:** Pig is a high-level platform for creating programs that run on Hadoop. It uses a language called Pig Latin, which simplifies the process of writing complex data transformations.

- **HBase:** HBase is a NoSQL database that runs on top of HDFS, providing real-time read/write access to large datasets. It is designed for random access to large amounts of sparse data.

- **Spark:** Apache Spark is an open-source data processing engine that can run on Hadoop. It provides in-memory processing capabilities, which significantly speeds up data processing tasks compared to traditional MapReduce.

Addressing Challenges in Big Data Processing

The growing Hadoop ecosystem addresses several challenges faced by organizations dealing with big data:

- **Data Variety:** With the explosion of data types, from structured to unstructured, the Hadoop ecosystem offers tools like Hive and Pig to handle diverse data formats seamlessly. This versatility allows organizations to process data from various sources, including social media, sensors, and transactional databases.

- **Scalability:** As data volumes continue to grow, scalability becomes a critical requirement. Hadoop's distributed architecture allows organizations to scale horizontally by adding more nodes to the cluster, thereby accommodating increased data loads without significant reconfiguration.

- **Real-time Processing:** Traditional batch processing methods can be slow and inefficient for time-sensitive applications. The integration of tools like Spark and HBase enables real-time data processing, allowing businesses to derive insights and make decisions promptly.

- **Data Governance and Security:** As organizations collect more data, ensuring data governance and security is paramount. Tools such as Apache Ranger and Apache Knox provide security features that help manage access controls and protect sensitive information within the Hadoop ecosystem.

Real-World Examples of Hadoop Ecosystem Applications

The effectiveness of the Hadoop ecosystem is illustrated through numerous real-world applications across various industries:

- **Retail Analytics:** Retail giants like Walmart utilize Hadoop to analyze customer purchase patterns, inventory management, and supply chain logistics. By processing terabytes of data, they can optimize pricing strategies and improve customer satisfaction.

- **Healthcare:** Healthcare organizations leverage Hadoop to analyze patient records, clinical trials, and medical imaging data. For instance, organizations like Mount Sinai have implemented Hadoop to enhance patient care through predictive analytics.

- **Financial Services:** Banks and financial institutions use Hadoop for fraud detection and risk management. By analyzing transaction data in real-time, they can identify suspicious activities and mitigate potential threats.
- **Social Media:** Companies like LinkedIn harness the power of Hadoop to analyze user interactions and engagement metrics. This analysis enables them to deliver personalized content and improve user experience.

The Future of the Hadoop Ecosystem

As the landscape of big data continues to evolve, the Hadoop ecosystem is poised for further growth and innovation. Emerging technologies such as artificial intelligence (AI) and machine learning (ML) are increasingly being integrated into the Hadoop framework, enhancing its capabilities for advanced analytics.

Furthermore, the rise of cloud computing has transformed how organizations deploy and manage their Hadoop clusters. With cloud-based solutions, businesses can leverage the scalability and flexibility of Hadoop without the need for extensive on-premises infrastructure.

In conclusion, the growing Hadoop ecosystem represents a powerful response to the challenges of big data processing. Through its diverse array of tools and technologies, it empowers organizations to harness the full potential of their data, driving innovation and informed decision-making across industries.

Challenges and Competitors

As Hadoop gained momentum in the big data ecosystem, it faced a myriad of challenges and competition from various emerging technologies and frameworks. Understanding these challenges is crucial for appreciating the impact and evolution of Hadoop in the data processing landscape.

1. Technical Challenges

Despite its innovative architecture, Hadoop encountered several technical challenges that threatened its usability and performance:

- **Data Locality:** Hadoop's design is predicated on the principle of data locality, which means processing should occur where the data resides. However, as data sets grew larger and more distributed, achieving optimal data locality became increasingly difficult. The inefficiencies in data movement led to increased latency and resource consumption, necessitating improvements in the Hadoop ecosystem.

- **Complexity of Configuration:** Hadoop's flexibility comes with complexity. Configuring a Hadoop cluster for optimal performance requires extensive knowledge of its components (e.g., HDFS, YARN, MapReduce). This steep learning curve often deterred new users and organizations from fully leveraging its capabilities.

- **Resource Management:** The original MapReduce model faced challenges in resource allocation, particularly in multi-tenant environments. As more applications began to share the same cluster, the need for a more sophisticated resource management system became evident. This led to the development of YARN (Yet Another Resource Negotiator), which enabled better resource allocation and management.

- **Data Processing Speed:** While Hadoop was revolutionary in handling large data sets, the batch processing model of MapReduce was not designed for real-time data processing. This limitation became apparent as businesses increasingly sought to analyze streaming data and respond to real-time events.

2. Competitive Landscape

The emergence of various competitors posed significant challenges to Hadoop's dominance. Some of the notable competitors include:

- **Apache Spark:** Spark emerged as a formidable competitor to Hadoop, particularly due to its in-memory processing capabilities, which allowed for faster data processing. Spark's ability to handle both batch and real-time data processing made it an attractive alternative for organizations seeking agility and performance. According to a study by Databricks, Spark can be up to 100 times faster than Hadoop for certain workloads, leading many organizations to adopt it over Hadoop.

- **Apache Flink:** Flink is another competitor that focuses on stream processing. It provides advanced features such as event time processing and stateful computations, making it suitable for complex event-driven applications. Organizations looking for real-time analytics and low-latency processing began to favor Flink for its capabilities.

- **NoSQL Databases:** Technologies like MongoDB, Cassandra, and HBase offered alternatives to Hadoop's HDFS for storing and managing large volumes of unstructured data. These NoSQL databases provided flexibility and scalability, allowing developers to model data without the constraints of a fixed schema, which was particularly appealing for agile development environments.

+ **Cloud-based Solutions:** The rise of cloud computing introduced services such as Amazon Redshift, Google BigQuery, and Azure Data Lake, which provided scalable data storage and analytics solutions without the overhead of managing on-premises Hadoop clusters. These services simplified data processing and storage, making them attractive to organizations looking to minimize infrastructure costs and complexity.

3. Market Adaptation

To remain competitive, the Hadoop ecosystem underwent significant adaptations:

+ **Ecosystem Expansion:** The Hadoop ecosystem expanded beyond just MapReduce and HDFS. Tools like Apache Hive, Apache Pig, and Apache HBase were developed to address specific use cases and improve usability. This diversification allowed Hadoop to cater to a broader range of data processing needs.

+ **Integration with Other Technologies:** Hadoop began integrating with other technologies to enhance its capabilities. For instance, the introduction of Apache Kafka for real-time data streaming and Apache NiFi for data flow management allowed Hadoop to handle both batch and streaming data seamlessly.

+ **Focus on User Experience:** To mitigate the complexity of configuration, various distributions of Hadoop, such as Cloudera and Hortonworks, emerged, providing user-friendly interfaces and tools for easier management and deployment. These distributions aimed to simplify the user experience and make Hadoop more accessible to organizations without extensive technical expertise.

4. Conclusion

In conclusion, while Hadoop pioneered the big data revolution, it faced numerous challenges and stiff competition from emerging technologies. The need for faster processing, real-time analytics, and user-friendly interfaces drove the evolution of Hadoop and the broader ecosystem. By adapting to these challenges and integrating new technologies, Hadoop has managed to maintain its relevance in the fast-evolving landscape of data processing, continuing to shape the future of big data analytics.

Beyond Hadoop: Doug Cutting's Contributions

Evolution of Hadoop

Improvements and New Features

The evolution of Hadoop is characterized by continuous improvements and the introduction of new features that cater to the ever-changing landscape of big data processing. From its inception, Hadoop has undergone a transformation that not only enhanced its performance but also expanded its capabilities to address a broader range of data processing challenges. This subsection delves into the key improvements and new features that have defined Hadoop's journey.

1. Enhanced Storage and Processing Capabilities

One of the most significant improvements in Hadoop has been its ability to handle larger datasets more efficiently. The introduction of the Hadoop Distributed File System (HDFS) allowed for the storage of massive amounts of data across clusters of commodity hardware. HDFS's architecture, which splits files into blocks and distributes them across nodes, ensures fault tolerance and high throughput.

The following equation illustrates the data distribution in HDFS:

$$D = \frac{N}{B} \tag{22}$$

Where:

- D = Data distribution efficiency

- N = Total number of nodes in the cluster

- B = Block size (default is 128 MB in newer versions)

This formula emphasizes how the efficiency of data distribution scales with the number of nodes, allowing Hadoop to process petabytes of data seamlessly.

2. Introduction of YARN

The introduction of Yet Another Resource Negotiator (YARN) in Hadoop 2.0 marked a pivotal shift in the architecture of Hadoop. Prior to YARN, Hadoop's processing capabilities were limited to the MapReduce model. YARN decouples resource management from data processing, enabling multiple data processing engines to run on a single cluster. This flexibility allows for various workloads, such as interactive queries and real-time analytics, to coexist with batch processing.

YARN's architecture is depicted as follows:

This diagram shows the ResourceManager, NodeManager, and ApplicationMaster components that collectively manage resources and scheduling, vastly improving cluster utilization.

3. Support for Multiple Programming Languages

Hadoop's evolution has also included support for multiple programming languages beyond Java, which was the original language for writing MapReduce jobs. With the introduction of Hadoop Streaming, developers can write MapReduce jobs in languages such as Python, Ruby, and R. This inclusivity has broadened the user base and allowed data scientists and analysts to leverage their existing skills in data processing.

4. Improved Data Processing Frameworks

The introduction of Apache Spark as a processing framework that runs on top of Hadoop has revolutionized data processing. Spark provides in-memory data processing capabilities, which significantly speeds up tasks compared to traditional MapReduce jobs. The following equation illustrates the performance improvement when using Spark:

$$T_{spark} = \frac{T_{mapreduce}}{S} \tag{23}$$

Where:

- T_{spark} = Time taken by Spark

EVOLUTION OF HADOOP

- $T_{mapreduce}$ = Time taken by MapReduce
- S = Speedup factor (typically between 10x to 100x for iterative algorithms)

This performance enhancement is crucial for applications that require quick insights from large datasets.

5. Security Enhancements

As Hadoop gained traction in enterprise environments, security became a paramount concern. The introduction of Kerberos authentication, along with the implementation of Access Control Lists (ACLs), has fortified Hadoop's security posture. These enhancements ensure that data is protected from unauthorized access while maintaining compliance with regulatory standards.

The security model can be summarized by the following components:

- **Authentication:** Ensures that users are who they claim to be.
- **Authorization:** Controls what authenticated users can do within the system.
- **Encryption:** Protects data at rest and in transit.

These security features have made Hadoop a viable option for processing sensitive data in industries such as finance and healthcare.

6. Improved Ecosystem Integration

Hadoop's ecosystem has seen significant improvements with the integration of various tools and frameworks. Tools like Apache Hive and Apache Pig simplify data querying and analysis, while Apache HBase provides a NoSQL database option for real-time data access. The integration of these tools allows for a more comprehensive data processing solution that caters to diverse analytical needs.

The following diagram illustrates the Hadoop ecosystem and its components:

This ecosystem enables users to choose the right tool for their specific data processing requirements, enhancing the overall usability of Hadoop.

7. Continuous Community Contributions

The open-source nature of Hadoop has fostered a vibrant community that continuously contributes to its improvement. Regular updates and enhancements are driven by user feedback and emerging technologies. This collaborative approach ensures that Hadoop remains relevant in the fast-paced world of big data.

In summary, the improvements and new features introduced in Hadoop have significantly elevated its status as a leading big data processing framework. From enhanced storage capabilities to security enhancements and ecosystem integrations, Hadoop has adapted to meet the needs of modern data processing challenges. As the landscape of data continues to evolve, so too will Hadoop, solidifying its legacy as a cornerstone of big data technology.

Hadoop's Journey to Apache Software Foundation

The journey of Hadoop to becoming a top-level project within the Apache Software Foundation (ASF) is a significant chapter in the evolution of open-source software. This transition not only marked a pivotal moment for Hadoop but also set a precedent for the development and governance of many other projects in the tech industry.

The Need for a Structured Governance Model

As Hadoop began to gain traction in the early 2000s, it became evident that a structured governance model was necessary to manage the growing community of developers and users. The open-source nature of Hadoop allowed for contributions from a wide array of individuals and organizations, but this also led to challenges in maintaining code quality, ensuring consistent updates, and fostering community engagement. The ASF provided a framework that addressed these concerns by establishing a formalized process for project management, which included guidelines for contributions, decision-making, and release cycles.

Initial Contributions and Community Building

Doug Cutting and his team recognized the importance of community in the success of Hadoop. The early adopters of Hadoop were not just developers; they were data scientists, researchers, and organizations looking for innovative solutions to handle massive datasets. As the user base expanded, Cutting actively encouraged contributions from diverse stakeholders. This approach not only enriched the project but also helped in cultivating a sense of ownership among contributors.

Becoming an Apache Incubator Project

In 2008, Hadoop entered the Apache Incubator, which is a crucial step for any project aspiring to become an official Apache project. The Incubator serves as a testing ground for new projects, allowing them to establish their community and

EVOLUTION OF HADOOP

governance practices under the ASF umbrella. During this phase, Hadoop underwent rigorous scrutiny to ensure that it adhered to the ASF's principles of meritocracy and community-driven development.

The Incubator phase also provided Hadoop with the necessary resources and exposure to a larger audience. The ASF's established infrastructure for mailing lists, issue tracking, and version control systems facilitated smoother collaboration among contributors. This period saw significant enhancements to Hadoop's architecture, including improvements in scalability and performance.

Graduation to Top-Level Project

In 2011, after demonstrating a robust community and a clear governance structure, Hadoop graduated from the Incubator to become a top-level project within the Apache Software Foundation. This milestone was not just a badge of honor; it was a testament to the hard work and dedication of the Hadoop community. The graduation signified that Hadoop had met the ASF's criteria for maturity, sustainability, and community engagement.

Upon graduation, Hadoop benefited from increased visibility and credibility in the tech industry. Major corporations, including Yahoo!, Facebook, and LinkedIn, began to adopt Hadoop for their big data needs, further solidifying its position as a leading solution for data processing.

Challenges Faced During the Journey

Despite its successes, Hadoop's journey to the ASF was not without challenges. One of the most significant hurdles was the need to maintain a balance between rapid development and stability. As new features were introduced, ensuring backward compatibility and system reliability became critical. The community had to navigate the complexities of version control and integration with existing systems, which required careful planning and coordination.

Moreover, as Hadoop's popularity grew, so did the number of forks and competing projects. The community faced the challenge of unifying efforts and preventing fragmentation, which could dilute the project's impact. The ASF's governance model helped mitigate these issues by providing a centralized platform for collaboration and decision-making.

Legacy and Impact on Open Source Projects

Hadoop's successful journey to the Apache Software Foundation has had a lasting impact on the open-source landscape. It set a benchmark for how projects can effectively manage community contributions while ensuring high standards of quality and governance. The lessons learned from Hadoop's experience have been instrumental in guiding other projects within the ASF and beyond.

The collaborative spirit fostered by Hadoop's community has also inspired a new generation of developers to engage with open-source projects, contributing their skills and creativity to solve real-world problems. This legacy continues to shape the future of software development, emphasizing the importance of collaboration, transparency, and community-driven innovation.

In conclusion, Hadoop's journey to the Apache Software Foundation exemplifies the power of community and structured governance in the open-source realm. It serves as a model for future projects aiming to navigate the complexities of software development and community engagement, ensuring that innovation thrives in an ever-evolving technological landscape.

Version Control and Updates

Version control is a critical aspect of software development that allows developers to manage changes to code, track modifications, and collaborate effectively. In the context of Hadoop, version control and updates played a significant role in its evolution and stability. This subsection delves into the theoretical foundations of version control, the problems encountered, and the solutions implemented in the Hadoop ecosystem.

Theoretical Foundations of Version Control

At its core, version control systems (VCS) provide a framework for managing changes to files over time. The two primary types of version control systems are:

- **Centralized Version Control Systems (CVCS):** In a CVCS, there is a single central repository where all versions of files are stored. Developers check out files from this central repository, make changes, and then check them back in. This model can lead to bottlenecks and challenges in collaboration.

- **Distributed Version Control Systems (DVCS):** In contrast, DVCS allows each developer to have a complete local copy of the repository, including its history. Changes can be made locally and later pushed to a central repository. This model enhances collaboration, as multiple developers can work on different features simultaneously without interfering with each other's work.

EVOLUTION OF HADOOP

Hadoop primarily utilizes a distributed version control system, which aligns well with its open-source nature and the collaborative efforts of its community. The most commonly used DVCS in the Hadoop ecosystem is Git.

Problems Encountered

As Hadoop evolved, several challenges emerged in managing version control and updates:

- **Complexity of Dependencies:** Hadoop is not a standalone project; it consists of multiple components, including HDFS, MapReduce, and YARN. Each component has its own versioning, and ensuring compatibility between these components became a significant challenge.

- **Frequent Updates:** The fast-paced development cycle led to frequent updates and releases. Keeping track of which version contained specific features or bug fixes required a robust versioning strategy.

- **User Adoption of New Versions:** With every new release, users faced the dilemma of whether to upgrade to the latest version or stick with a stable release. This decision was often complicated by the need for testing and validation in production environments.

Solutions Implemented

To address these challenges, the Hadoop community implemented several solutions:

- **Semantic Versioning:** Hadoop adopted semantic versioning (SemVer) to provide clarity on the nature of changes in each release. The version number is structured as MAJOR.MINOR.PATCH, where:

    - MAJOR version increments indicate incompatible API changes,
    - MINOR version increments represent backward-compatible functionality, and
    - PATCH version increments are for backward-compatible bug fixes.

    This structured approach helped users understand the implications of upgrading to a new version.

- **Release Notes and Documentation:** Comprehensive release notes were created for each version, detailing new features, bug fixes, and any breaking changes. This documentation became an essential resource for users to make informed decisions about upgrades.

- **Branching Strategies:** The use of branching strategies in Git allowed developers to work on new features or bug fixes in isolation from the main codebase. This approach minimized disruptions to the stable version while enabling continuous development.

- **Automated Testing and Continuous Integration:** To ensure the stability of new versions, the Hadoop community implemented automated testing and continuous integration (CI) practices. This allowed developers to catch issues early in the development cycle, reducing the risk of introducing bugs in production releases.

Examples of Version Control in Hadoop

A notable example of effective version control in Hadoop is the transition from Hadoop 1.x to 2.x. This transition introduced significant architectural changes, including the introduction of YARN (Yet Another Resource Negotiator). The community followed a structured versioning approach to manage this transition:

- The release of Hadoop 2.0.0-alpha marked the beginning of the new architecture, allowing users to test and provide feedback.

- Subsequent releases, such as 2.2.0 and 2.3.0, included enhancements and optimizations based on user feedback and testing results.

- The careful management of version control during this transition ensured that users could gradually adopt the new features without disrupting their existing workflows.

In conclusion, version control and updates are pivotal in the evolution of Hadoop. By adopting a robust versioning strategy, addressing challenges effectively, and implementing best practices in collaboration, the Hadoop community has ensured that the project remains resilient and adaptable to the ever-changing landscape of big data technologies. The lessons learned from Hadoop's version control journey continue to influence best practices in software development across the industry.

Hadoop's Integration into Other Systems

Hadoop, an open-source framework designed for distributed storage and processing of large data sets, has become a cornerstone of modern data architecture. Its ability to integrate seamlessly into various systems has played a crucial role in its widespread adoption across industries. This section delves into the mechanisms of Hadoop's integration, the challenges encountered, and the solutions that have emerged to facilitate its interoperability with other technologies.

Understanding Integration Mechanisms

Hadoop's architecture is inherently modular, consisting of several components that can operate independently or in conjunction with other systems. The core components include the Hadoop Distributed File System (HDFS), the MapReduce processing model, and the YARN resource management layer. The integration of these components with external systems is achieved through several methods:

- **APIs:** Hadoop provides a set of APIs that allow developers to interact with its components programmatically. For instance, the Hadoop FileSystem API enables applications to read and write data to HDFS, while the MapReduce API allows for the execution of distributed processing tasks.

- **Connectors:** Various connectors have been developed to facilitate integration with popular data storage and processing systems. For example, the Hadoop ecosystem includes connectors for databases like Apache HBase, NoSQL databases like MongoDB, and data warehousing solutions like Apache Hive.

- **Data Ingestion Tools:** Tools such as Apache Flume and Apache Sqoop are designed to help ingest data from various sources into Hadoop. Flume is particularly useful for streaming data, while Sqoop is tailored for transferring bulk data between Hadoop and relational databases.

Challenges of Integration

While Hadoop's flexibility offers numerous integration possibilities, several challenges can arise during the process:

- **Data Format Compatibility:** Different systems often use distinct data formats. For instance, relational databases typically utilize structured data, while Hadoop can handle both structured and unstructured data. This disparity can complicate data transfers and processing.

- **Performance Issues:** Integrating Hadoop with other systems can introduce latency, especially when dealing with large volumes of data. The performance overhead associated with data serialization and network communication can become significant, impacting overall system efficiency.

- **Security Concerns:** As Hadoop integrates with various systems, ensuring data security and compliance becomes paramount. Data breaches can occur during transfers, necessitating robust authentication and encryption mechanisms.

Solutions and Examples

To address these challenges, several strategies and tools have emerged:

- **Data Serialization Formats:** To improve data format compatibility, serialization formats like Avro and Parquet have been adopted. These formats allow for efficient data serialization and deserialization, enabling seamless data exchange between systems. Avro, for example, supports schema evolution, making it easier to handle changes in data structure.

$$\text{Efficiency} = \frac{\text{Data Size}}{\text{Serialization Time}} \quad \text{(in bytes/second)} \qquad (24)$$

This equation illustrates how efficiency can be quantified in terms of data size and serialization time.

- **Data Processing Frameworks:** Frameworks like Apache Spark can be integrated with Hadoop to enhance performance. Spark's in-memory processing capabilities allow for faster data processing compared to Hadoop's traditional disk-based MapReduce model.

$$\text{Speedup} = \frac{\text{Time}_{\text{Hadoop}}}{\text{Time}_{\text{Spark}}} \qquad (25)$$

This formula quantifies the performance improvement achieved by using Spark over Hadoop.

- **Security Protocols:** To mitigate security risks, Hadoop has incorporated various security measures, including Kerberos authentication and data encryption. These protocols help ensure that data remains secure during transfers and while stored in HDFS.

Case Studies

Several organizations have successfully integrated Hadoop with other systems, showcasing the framework's versatility:

- **LinkedIn:** LinkedIn utilizes Hadoop for its data processing needs, integrating it with Kafka for real-time data streaming. This integration allows LinkedIn to analyze user interactions and provide personalized content recommendations.

- **Spotify:** Spotify employs Hadoop in conjunction with Apache Spark to process vast amounts of user data. By integrating these technologies, Spotify can deliver real-time insights into user behavior, enhancing its recommendation algorithms.

- **Yahoo:** As one of the early adopters of Hadoop, Yahoo integrated it with various data sources, including relational databases and NoSQL stores. This integration enabled Yahoo to build a robust data processing pipeline that supports its diverse applications.

Conclusion

Hadoop's ability to integrate into a variety of systems has been pivotal in its rise as a dominant force in the big data landscape. Despite the challenges associated with integration, the development of robust tools and frameworks has paved the way for successful implementations across industries. As data continues to grow in volume and complexity, Hadoop's role in facilitating seamless integration will remain vital, ensuring that organizations can harness the power of data to drive innovation and decision-making.

In summary, Hadoop's integration into other systems not only enhances its functionality but also broadens its applicability, making it an indispensable tool in the modern data ecosystem.

Balancing Innovation and Stability

In the fast-paced world of technology, particularly in the realm of open-source software development, the challenge of balancing innovation with stability is a critical concern. For Doug Cutting, this balance was not merely a theoretical consideration but a practical necessity as he navigated the evolution of Hadoop. The duality of fostering groundbreaking advancements while ensuring reliable and stable software is a delicate dance that requires foresight, strategic planning, and community engagement.

The Nature of Innovation and Stability

Innovation in software can be defined as the introduction of new ideas, features, or methodologies that enhance functionality or performance. Conversely, stability refers to the reliability, predictability, and robustness of software systems, ensuring that they perform their intended functions without failure. In the context of Hadoop, innovation may involve adding new processing capabilities or integrating with emerging technologies, while stability ensures that existing functionalities remain intact and that users can depend on the system for critical operations.

The relationship between innovation and stability can be modeled using a simple equation:

$$\text{Success} = \frac{\text{Innovation}}{\text{Instability}} \quad (26)$$

This equation suggests that as innovation increases, the potential for success grows; however, if instability rises too high, it can negate the benefits of innovation. Thus, the goal is to maximize innovation while minimizing instability.

Challenges in Balancing Innovation and Stability

One of the primary challenges in balancing innovation and stability is the introduction of new features. Each new feature has the potential to disrupt existing functionality, leading to bugs and performance issues. For example, when Hadoop introduced YARN (Yet Another Resource Negotiator) as a resource management layer, it was essential to ensure that this innovation did not compromise the core functionalities of the existing MapReduce framework. The integration of YARN required extensive testing and validation to ensure that it enhanced the system without introducing critical failures.

Another challenge arises from the diverse user base of Hadoop, which spans various industries and applications. Different users may have varying requirements

EVOLUTION OF HADOOP

for stability and innovation. For instance, a financial institution might prioritize stability due to regulatory compliance, while a startup may be more focused on rapid innovation to gain a competitive edge. This disparity necessitates a careful approach to feature releases, often requiring a phased rollout strategy to accommodate different user needs.

Strategies for Achieving Balance

To effectively balance innovation and stability, Doug Cutting and the Hadoop community employed several strategies:

- **Versioning and Backward Compatibility:** Each new release of Hadoop is meticulously designed to maintain backward compatibility with previous versions. This ensures that existing applications continue to function as expected, even as new features are introduced. The semantic versioning system allows users to anticipate the impact of upgrades, helping them manage their deployment strategies.

- **Extensive Testing Protocols:** Rigorous testing is a cornerstone of Hadoop's development process. The community utilizes automated testing frameworks to run extensive test suites that cover various scenarios, ensuring that new features do not inadvertently break existing functionality. This practice is complemented by user feedback during beta testing phases, which helps identify potential issues before a full release.

- **Community Engagement and Collaboration:** The open-source nature of Hadoop fosters a collaborative environment where developers, users, and stakeholders can contribute to the project's direction. Engaging the community in discussions about upcoming features and their potential impact allows for a more democratic approach to innovation, where stability concerns can be voiced and addressed before implementation.

- **Incremental Releases:** Instead of large, sweeping updates, the Hadoop community favors incremental releases that introduce new features gradually. This approach allows users to adapt to changes more easily and provides an opportunity to assess the impact of innovations in a controlled manner. For example, the introduction of new storage formats or processing models can be rolled out as optional features, giving users the choice to adopt them at their own pace.

Real-World Examples

The evolution of Hadoop provides several real-world examples of how balancing innovation and stability has been successfully achieved:

- **Hadoop 2.0 and YARN:** The release of Hadoop 2.0 marked a significant shift in the architecture with the introduction of YARN. This innovation allowed for more efficient resource management and the ability to run different processing frameworks on top of Hadoop. The community took great care to ensure that existing MapReduce applications continued to function seamlessly, demonstrating a successful balance between groundbreaking innovation and maintaining stability.

- **Hadoop Ecosystem Growth:** As the Hadoop ecosystem expanded with projects like Apache Spark, Hive, and HBase, the challenge of integration arose. Each new project brought innovative capabilities, but also the risk of introducing instability. The Hadoop community addressed this by establishing clear guidelines for integration and ensuring that all components adhered to rigorous stability standards before being incorporated into the ecosystem.

Conclusion

In conclusion, the balance between innovation and stability is a fundamental aspect of Doug Cutting's approach to developing Hadoop. By implementing strategies such as versioning, extensive testing, community engagement, and incremental releases, the Hadoop community has successfully navigated the complexities of software evolution. As technology continues to advance, this balance will remain crucial for fostering a robust and innovative data processing ecosystem that meets the diverse needs of its users. The lessons learned from Hadoop's journey serve as a valuable guide for future software development endeavors, highlighting the importance of maintaining stability while pursuing innovative solutions.

Other Notable Projects and Collaborations

Lucene and Search Technologies

Apache Lucene is a powerful, open-source search library that has revolutionized the way we approach information retrieval. Developed by Doug Cutting, Lucene provides a robust framework for implementing search capabilities in applications,

OTHER NOTABLE PROJECTS AND COLLABORATIONS

enabling developers to build sophisticated search engines with relative ease. This section explores the foundational concepts of Lucene, its architecture, and the challenges it addresses in the realm of search technologies.

Theoretical Foundations of Information Retrieval

At its core, information retrieval (IR) is the process of obtaining information system resources that are relevant to an information need from a collection of those resources. Theories of IR are grounded in several key principles, including:

- **Boolean Retrieval Model:** This model uses Boolean logic to match documents with queries. A query is formed using operators such as AND, OR, and NOT. While simple, this model can lead to issues with recall and precision.

- **Vector Space Model:** This model represents documents and queries as vectors in a multi-dimensional space. Similarity between documents and queries is computed using cosine similarity, allowing for ranked retrieval.

- **Probabilistic Model:** This approach estimates the probability that a given document is relevant to a query. The BM25 algorithm is a widely used probabilistic model that adjusts term frequency and inverse document frequency to rank documents.

Lucene Architecture

Lucene's architecture is designed to facilitate efficient indexing and searching. The main components include:

- **Indexing:** Lucene creates an inverted index that maps terms to their locations in documents. This structure allows for fast lookups. The indexing process involves tokenization, normalization, and the creation of postings lists.

- **Search:** When a search query is executed, Lucene retrieves matching documents from the inverted index. It employs scoring algorithms to rank results based on relevance.

- **Analyzer:** Analyzers are responsible for processing text during both indexing and searching. They handle tasks such as tokenization, stemming, and removing stop words.

The following equation illustrates the scoring function used in Lucene:

$$\text{score}(d, q) = \sum_{t \in q} \text{tf}(t, d) \cdot \text{idf}(t) \qquad (27)$$

Where: - d is a document, - q is a query, - $\text{tf}(t, d)$ is the term frequency of term t in document d, - $\text{idf}(t)$ is the inverse document frequency of term t.

Challenges in Search Technologies

Despite its power, Lucene faces several challenges in the domain of search technologies:

- **Scalability:** As the volume of data grows, maintaining performance becomes crucial. Lucene must efficiently handle large indexes and high query loads.

- **Relevance Tuning:** Achieving high relevance in search results requires continuous tuning of scoring algorithms and analyzers. This can be a complex process, especially in diverse datasets.

- **Handling Multilingual Data:** Supporting multiple languages introduces additional complexity in tokenization and stemming. Lucene provides language-specific analyzers, but challenges remain in ensuring consistent performance across languages.

Examples of Lucene Applications

Lucene's versatility allows it to be integrated into various applications, including:

- **Content Management Systems (CMS):** Many CMS platforms utilize Lucene for robust search capabilities, enabling users to find content quickly and efficiently.

- **E-commerce:** Online retailers implement Lucene to enhance product search, allowing customers to filter results based on various attributes and preferences.

- **Enterprise Search:** Organizations leverage Lucene to provide search functionality across internal documents, emails, and databases, improving information accessibility.

Conclusion

Lucene stands as a testament to Doug Cutting's vision of democratizing access to information. By providing a powerful, open-source search library, Lucene has empowered developers to create advanced search solutions across various domains. As the landscape of data continues to evolve, Lucene remains at the forefront of search technologies, addressing challenges and pushing the boundaries of what is possible in information retrieval.

In summary, the journey of Lucene from a simple search library to a cornerstone of modern search technologies exemplifies the impact of innovative thinking in software development. Its ongoing evolution and community support ensure that it will continue to play a significant role in the future of search.

Nutch and Web Search

Nutch is an open-source web crawler software project that Doug Cutting co-founded, which plays a pivotal role in the landscape of web search technologies. The inception of Nutch was driven by the need for a scalable and flexible solution to index the vast expanse of the internet. As the web grew exponentially in the early 2000s, traditional search engines struggled to keep pace with the volume and diversity of data available online. Nutch emerged as a response to these challenges, providing a framework that could be adapted to various use cases in web crawling and search.

The Architecture of Nutch

At its core, Nutch is built on a modular architecture that allows developers to customize and extend its functionalities. The main components of Nutch include:

- **Crawler:** The crawler is responsible for fetching web pages. It utilizes a set of configurable parameters to determine the depth and breadth of the crawling process.

- **Parser:** After fetching the content, the parser extracts relevant information from the HTML pages. This includes metadata, links, and the body text, which is essential for indexing.

- **Indexer:** The indexer processes the parsed data and stores it in a searchable format. Nutch can integrate with various indexing backends, including Apache Lucene, to facilitate efficient search operations.

- **Query Interface:** This component allows users to perform searches against the indexed data. It can be tailored to meet specific user requirements and can support advanced search features.

The following equation illustrates the relationship between the number of pages crawled N, the depth of crawling D, and the average number of links per page L:

$$N = L^D$$

This exponential growth highlights the potential for a crawler like Nutch to index a significant portion of the web, given sufficient time and resources.

Challenges in Web Crawling

Developing an effective web crawler is not without its challenges. Nutch faced several hurdles during its development, including:

- **Robots.txt Compliance:** Many websites use the robots.txt file to specify which parts of their site should not be crawled. Nutch must respect these directives to avoid legal and ethical issues.
- **Dynamic Content:** Modern websites often rely on JavaScript to load content dynamically. Crawling such sites requires advanced techniques to ensure that the crawler captures all relevant information.
- **Scalability:** As the web continues to grow, Nutch needed to implement distributed crawling capabilities to manage the increasing volume of data efficiently. This led to the integration of Hadoop, allowing Nutch to scale horizontally across multiple nodes.

Use Cases of Nutch in Web Search

Nutch has found numerous applications in the realm of web search. Some notable use cases include:

- **Academic Research:** Universities and research institutions have utilized Nutch to create specialized search engines for academic publications, enabling researchers to discover relevant literature more efficiently.
- **Enterprise Search:** Organizations have deployed Nutch to index their internal documents, emails, and other resources, providing employees with powerful search capabilities to enhance productivity.

- **Custom Search Engines:** Developers have leveraged Nutch to build tailored search engines for niche markets, allowing businesses to focus on specific content areas and improve user experience.

For instance, a university might configure Nutch to crawl and index only academic journals and conference proceedings, providing students and faculty with a dedicated search tool that filters out irrelevant content.

Integration with Other Technologies

Nutch's flexibility allows it to integrate with other technologies to enhance its capabilities. One of the most significant integrations is with Apache Solr, a powerful search platform built on top of Apache Lucene. By connecting Nutch with Solr, users can benefit from advanced search features such as faceting, filtering, and real-time indexing. This combination empowers organizations to create robust search solutions tailored to their specific needs.

Conclusion

Nutch represents a significant milestone in the evolution of web search technologies. Its open-source nature and modular architecture have made it a valuable tool for developers and organizations looking to harness the power of web data. By addressing the challenges of web crawling and indexing, Nutch has paved the way for innovative search solutions that continue to evolve alongside the internet. Doug Cutting's vision for Nutch not only transformed how we approach web search but also laid the groundwork for future advancements in data processing and analytics.

Contributions to Apache Software Foundation

Doug Cutting's journey through the tech world is intrinsically linked to the Apache Software Foundation (ASF), an organization that has become synonymous with open-source development. His contributions to the ASF have not only shaped his career but have also profoundly influenced the landscape of software engineering and big data analytics.

Foundational Role in ASF

The Apache Software Foundation was established in 1999, and it quickly became a beacon for open-source projects, fostering a community-driven approach to software development. Doug Cutting's involvement with ASF began with the creation of the Apache Lucene project, a powerful search library that has become a cornerstone for various search applications. Lucene's architecture is based on the inverted index, a data structure that allows for fast full-text searches. The effectiveness of Lucene can be summarized by the equation:

$$\text{Search Time} = O(\log n)$$

where n is the number of documents indexed. This logarithmic search time is a significant improvement over linear search methods, making Lucene highly efficient for large datasets.

Hadoop and the ASF Ecosystem

Following the success of Lucene, Doug Cutting recognized the need for a distributed computing framework capable of handling vast amounts of data. This recognition led to the inception of Hadoop, which was initially inspired by Google's MapReduce and Google File System papers. Hadoop's architecture allows for the processing of large datasets across clusters of computers using simple programming models. The core components of Hadoop are:

1. **Hadoop Distributed File System (HDFS)**: A distributed file system designed to run on commodity hardware. HDFS is fault-tolerant and provides high-throughput access to application data.
2. **MapReduce**: A programming model for processing large data sets with a distributed algorithm on a cluster.
3. **YARN (Yet Another Resource Negotiator)**: A resource management layer for Hadoop that allows multiple data processing engines to handle data stored in a single platform.

The introduction of these components to the ASF ecosystem marked a significant turning point in how data processing was approached. The ability to process petabytes of data efficiently opened new avenues for data science, analytics, and machine learning.

Community Engagement and Leadership

Doug Cutting's leadership style has been characterized by his emphasis on community engagement. He believes that the strength of open-source projects lies in their communities. This philosophy is encapsulated in the ASF's guiding principles, which include meritocracy and consensus-driven development. Cutting has actively promoted these values within the Hadoop community, fostering an environment where contributors feel valued and empowered to innovate.

For example, during the early development of Hadoop, Cutting organized meetups and conferences, such as the Hadoop Summit, to bring together developers, users, and industry leaders. These gatherings facilitated knowledge sharing and collaboration, which were crucial for the project's growth. The impact of community-driven development can be illustrated through the increased adoption rates of Hadoop, as evidenced by the following statistics:

- In 2011, Hadoop was used by approximately 10% of Fortune 500 companies.
- By 2020, that number had surged to over 60%, demonstrating the framework's widespread acceptance and integration into enterprise solutions.

Advocating for Open Source Principles

Throughout his career, Doug Cutting has been a staunch advocate for open-source principles. He has frequently spoken about the importance of transparency, collaboration, and accessibility in software development. His contributions to the ASF embody these principles, as he has consistently championed the idea that great software should be available to everyone, not just those who can afford it.

This advocacy is evident in the way he has approached project management within the ASF. For instance, he has been instrumental in ensuring that all decisions regarding Hadoop's development are made openly, allowing for community input and feedback. This practice not only enhances the quality of the software but also builds trust within the community.

Educational Impact and Mentorship

In addition to his technical contributions, Doug Cutting has played a vital role in mentoring the next generation of software developers and data scientists. He has participated in numerous educational initiatives, including workshops, webinars, and university lectures, where he shares his insights on open-source development and the importance of community involvement.

Cutting's mentorship extends beyond just technical skills; he emphasizes the importance of soft skills such as communication, collaboration, and problem-solving. He often advises aspiring developers to engage with open-source projects, as this experience can provide invaluable learning opportunities and help them build a robust professional network.

Legacy and Future Directions

Doug Cutting's contributions to the Apache Software Foundation have left an indelible mark on the tech industry. His work has not only advanced the field of big data but has also set a standard for open-source development practices. As the landscape of technology continues to evolve, Cutting's influence will undoubtedly persist, inspiring future generations of developers to embrace collaboration, innovation, and the open-source ethos.

In conclusion, Doug Cutting's journey within the Apache Software Foundation serves as a testament to the power of community-driven development and the significant impact that one individual can have on an entire industry. His contributions have reshaped how we think about data processing, and his legacy will continue to inspire those who follow in his footsteps.

Partnerships and Industry Influence

Doug Cutting's journey through the tech landscape is not just a story of individual brilliance; it is also a narrative deeply intertwined with strategic partnerships and significant industry influence. These collaborations have played a critical role in shaping the trajectory of Hadoop and the broader open-source ecosystem.

The Importance of Collaborations

In the tech industry, partnerships often serve as catalysts for innovation. Doug understood early on that collaboration could amplify the impact of his work. By engaging with other developers, researchers, and organizations, he was able to harness diverse perspectives and expertise. This collaborative spirit was particularly evident during the formative years of Hadoop, where contributions from various stakeholders helped refine the framework.

Key Partnerships in Hadoop's Development

One of the most notable partnerships was with Yahoo!, where Doug Cutting and his team were given the resources to develop Hadoop further. Yahoo! was facing massive data challenges, and they needed a scalable solution to manage their growing datasets. By aligning their needs with Cutting's vision, they created a symbiotic relationship that not only advanced Hadoop but also positioned Yahoo! as a leader in big data processing.

This partnership was crucial for several reasons:

OTHER NOTABLE PROJECTS AND COLLABORATIONS

- **Resource Allocation:** Yahoo! provided the necessary infrastructure and financial backing for the development of Hadoop, allowing Cutting to focus on innovation without the constraints of limited resources.

- **Real-World Testing:** The partnership allowed for real-world applications of Hadoop, facilitating immediate feedback and iterative improvements based on actual performance metrics.

- **Community Building:** Yahoo! helped to foster a community around Hadoop, encouraging other developers to contribute and share their insights, which ultimately enriched the project.

Influence on the Open Source Community

Doug Cutting's commitment to open source was not merely a personal philosophy; it was a strategic approach that influenced the entire tech industry. By making Hadoop available to the public, he invited developers from around the world to contribute to its growth. This open-source model democratized access to advanced data processing technologies, allowing smaller companies and startups to leverage Hadoop without the burden of hefty licensing fees.

The impact of this decision was profound:

$$\text{Innovation} = \text{Community Contribution} + \text{Open Access} \quad (28)$$

As more developers engaged with Hadoop, they brought unique challenges and solutions that further propelled the technology's evolution. This collaborative ecosystem led to the creation of various Hadoop-related projects, such as Hive for data warehousing and Pig for data flow scripting, showcasing how partnerships can yield additional layers of innovation.

Industry Influence and Recognition

The influence of Doug Cutting and Hadoop extended beyond just technical advancements; it reshaped industry standards and practices. Companies began to recognize the value of open-source solutions as viable alternatives to proprietary software. This shift in perception was instrumental in fostering a culture of collaboration and knowledge sharing within the tech community.

For instance, major corporations like Facebook, LinkedIn, and Twitter adopted Hadoop for their data processing needs, further validating its effectiveness. These companies not only utilized Hadoop but also contributed back to the project, enhancing its capabilities and ensuring its relevance in an ever-evolving tech landscape.

The recognition of Hadoop's impact was also reflected in various awards and accolades, such as:

- **The InfoWorld Technology of the Year Award** for its contributions to big data processing.
- **The Jolt Product Excellence Award** recognizing its innovative approach to data management.
- **Recognition at industry conferences** like Strata and Hadoop Summit, where Doug Cutting often shared the stage with other tech luminaries, further solidifying his influence.

Challenges in Partnerships

Despite the successes, partnerships also came with their own set of challenges. Aligning the interests of various stakeholders can be difficult, and there were instances where conflicting priorities threatened to derail progress. For example, as Hadoop gained traction, the influx of contributions from different organizations led to debates over governance and direction.

To address these challenges, Doug Cutting emphasized the importance of clear communication and a shared vision. By fostering an inclusive environment where all voices were heard, he was able to navigate the complexities of collaboration while maintaining the integrity of the project.

Conclusion

In conclusion, Doug Cutting's partnerships and industry influence were pivotal in the development and success of Hadoop. Through strategic collaborations, he not only advanced his vision but also transformed the tech landscape, fostering a culture of open-source innovation that continues to thrive today. The story of Hadoop serves as a testament to the power of collaboration, showcasing how partnerships can drive technological advancement and create lasting impact in the industry.

Doug's Legacy in Open Source Community

Doug Cutting's influence in the realm of open source software is both profound and multifaceted. His contributions have not only shaped the trajectory of

OTHER NOTABLE PROJECTS AND COLLABORATIONS

numerous technologies but have also fostered a culture of collaboration, innovation, and accessibility within the tech community. This section delves into the various dimensions of Doug's legacy in the open source community, highlighting key projects, philosophies, and the lasting impact he has made.

The Philosophy of Open Source

At the core of Doug Cutting's contributions is a steadfast belief in the principles of open source. This philosophy advocates for transparency, collaboration, and shared knowledge, allowing developers from around the world to contribute to and benefit from collective advancements. Doug has often articulated that open source is not merely a licensing model but a movement towards democratizing technology. This ethos has been instrumental in shaping the culture of many projects he has been involved with, including Hadoop, Lucene, and Nutch.

Hadoop: A Catalyst for Change

Hadoop, perhaps Doug's most significant contribution, exemplifies the open source ethos in action. Launched in 2005, Hadoop was designed to tackle the challenges of big data processing, enabling organizations to store and analyze massive datasets efficiently. Its architecture, based on the MapReduce programming model, allowed for distributed processing across clusters of computers, which was revolutionary at the time.

The decision to release Hadoop as an open source project under the Apache Software Foundation was pivotal. This move not only accelerated its adoption but also encouraged a vibrant community of contributors. As a result, Hadoop became a cornerstone for many data-driven applications and services, empowering industries ranging from finance to healthcare to harness the power of data analytics.

Community Engagement and Collaboration

Doug's approach to community engagement is another facet of his legacy. He has consistently emphasized the importance of collaboration among developers, users, and organizations. By fostering an inclusive environment, Doug has encouraged individuals from diverse backgrounds to contribute to open source projects, thus enriching the community with varied perspectives and expertise.

For instance, the Hadoop ecosystem has grown to include numerous projects, such as Apache Hive, Apache Pig, and Apache Spark, all of which have stemmed from the foundational work of Hadoop. This expansion is a testament to the collaborative spirit that Doug has nurtured. The Hadoop community hosts regular meetups, conferences, and hackathons, allowing developers to share knowledge, solve problems, and innovate together.

Educational Initiatives and Mentorship

Doug Cutting's legacy extends beyond code and projects; it encompasses his commitment to education and mentorship within the open source community. He has been an advocate for teaching programming and data science skills to the next generation of developers. By participating in workshops, giving talks, and mentoring aspiring technologists, Doug has played a crucial role in shaping the skills and mindset of future contributors to open source.

One notable initiative is the Apache Software Foundation's mentorship program, which Doug has supported. This program aims to connect experienced developers with newcomers, facilitating knowledge transfer and skill development. Such efforts are vital in ensuring the sustainability and growth of the open source community.

Recognition and Influence

Doug Cutting's contributions to open source have not gone unnoticed. He has received numerous accolades for his work, including recognition from the technology industry and academic institutions. His influence can be seen in the widespread adoption of open source practices across various sectors. Companies now recognize the value of open source not only for cost savings but also for innovation and agility.

Moreover, Doug's work has inspired countless developers to contribute to open source projects. By exemplifying the impact of collaborative development, he has motivated others to engage with the community, thus perpetuating a cycle of innovation and growth. The success of projects like Apache Hadoop serves as a blueprint for future open source endeavors, demonstrating the potential of collective effort in solving complex problems.

Challenges and Future Directions

Despite the successes, Doug's journey in the open source community has not been without challenges. Issues such as maintaining project sustainability, ensuring diversity within the community, and navigating the complexities of corporate involvement in open source have posed significant hurdles. Doug has been vocal about these challenges, advocating for practices that promote inclusivity and sustainability.

Looking forward, Doug's legacy will continue to influence the evolution of open source software. As technology advances and new challenges arise, the principles he championed will remain relevant. The need for scalable, efficient, and accessible solutions in data processing will drive the next generation of open source projects, with Doug's foundational work serving as a guiding light.

In conclusion, Doug Cutting's legacy in the open source community is characterized by his unwavering commitment to collaboration, education, and innovation. Through his work on Hadoop and other projects, he has transformed the landscape of technology, empowering individuals and organizations alike. As the open source movement continues to evolve, Doug's contributions will undoubtedly inspire future generations of developers to embrace the spirit of collaboration and make their mark on the world of technology.

Challenges and Successes

Overcoming Technical Obstacles

Scaling Hadoop for Enterprise-level Workloads

In the rapidly evolving landscape of big data, the ability to scale systems efficiently is paramount. Hadoop, an open-source framework designed for distributed storage and processing of large datasets, was conceived with scalability in mind. However, as enterprises began to adopt Hadoop for their data-intensive applications, challenges arose that required innovative solutions to ensure that Hadoop could handle enterprise-level workloads effectively.

Understanding Enterprise-level Workloads

Enterprise-level workloads refer to the vast and complex data processing tasks that organizations face, often characterized by high volume, velocity, and variety. These workloads can include batch processing of large datasets, real-time analytics, and machine learning model training. To effectively manage these tasks, Hadoop must not only store large amounts of data but also process it quickly and reliably.

Challenges in Scaling Hadoop

Scaling Hadoop for enterprise workloads presents several challenges:

- **Data Volume:** As organizations generate and collect more data, the sheer volume can overwhelm traditional systems. Hadoop's distributed architecture allows it to handle vast amounts of data, but managing this data efficiently requires careful planning.

- **Data Variety:** Enterprises often deal with structured, semi-structured, and unstructured data. Hadoop's ability to process different data formats is a strength, yet it complicates the architecture and necessitates robust data governance.

- **Data Velocity:** The speed at which data is generated and needs to be processed is critical. For instance, real-time analytics on streaming data requires Hadoop to be integrated with tools like Apache Kafka and Apache Storm, which can complicate the architecture.

- **Resource Management:** As workloads grow, efficiently managing resources such as CPU, memory, and disk I/O becomes essential. Hadoop's default resource management system, YARN (Yet Another Resource Negotiator), plays a crucial role in addressing this challenge.

The Role of YARN in Scaling

YARN was introduced in Hadoop 2.0 to address scalability issues inherent in earlier versions. By separating resource management from data processing, YARN allows multiple applications to run on a Hadoop cluster simultaneously. This modular approach enhances scalability and flexibility, enabling organizations to allocate resources dynamically based on workload demands.

The architecture of YARN consists of three main components:

- **ResourceManager (RM):** This master daemon manages the cluster resources and schedules applications.

- **NodeManager (NM):** Each node in the cluster runs a NodeManager, which is responsible for monitoring resource usage on that node and reporting it to the ResourceManager.

- **ApplicationMaster (AM):** For each application, an ApplicationMaster negotiates resources from the ResourceManager and works with the NodeManagers to execute and monitor the tasks.

This architecture allows Hadoop to scale horizontally by adding more nodes to the cluster, which can handle more data and more concurrent applications without a significant drop in performance.

Techniques for Efficient Scaling

To scale Hadoop effectively for enterprise workloads, organizations have adopted several techniques:

- **Data Partitioning:** By dividing data into smaller, manageable chunks (partitions), Hadoop can distribute the load across the cluster more evenly. This approach minimizes bottlenecks and maximizes throughput.

- **Replication:** Hadoop employs a replication strategy to ensure data durability and availability. By default, each data block is replicated three times across different nodes. This redundancy not only protects against data loss but also enhances read performance.

- **Compression:** Reducing the size of data stored in HDFS (Hadoop Distributed File System) through compression techniques can significantly improve I/O performance. Compression reduces the amount of data transferred over the network and speeds up processing times.

- **Tuning Configuration:** Fine-tuning Hadoop's configuration settings based on the specific workload can lead to substantial performance improvements. Parameters such as block size, replication factor, and memory allocation should be adjusted according to the needs of the enterprise.

Case Study: A Retail Giant's Hadoop Implementation

Consider a leading retail company that implemented Hadoop to manage its vast amounts of customer data and transaction records. Initially, the company faced challenges with data processing speed and resource allocation, leading to delays in generating actionable insights.

To address these issues, the company adopted the following strategies:

- They increased the cluster size from 50 to 200 nodes, allowing for greater parallel processing capabilities.

- Implemented YARN to manage resources more effectively, enabling multiple teams to run their data processing jobs simultaneously without interference.

- Employed data partitioning strategies to segment customer data by region, which improved query performance and reduced processing times.

As a result, the retail giant was able to reduce the time taken to generate reports from days to hours, significantly enhancing their ability to respond to market trends and customer needs.

Conclusion

Scaling Hadoop for enterprise-level workloads is a multifaceted challenge that requires a deep understanding of both the technology and the specific needs of the organization. By leveraging YARN, implementing effective data management strategies, and continuously tuning system configurations, enterprises can harness the full power of Hadoop to drive innovation and gain a competitive edge in the data-driven economy. As organizations continue to evolve, the scalability of Hadoop will remain a critical factor in their success.

Handling Varying Data Types and Formats

In the realm of big data, one of the most significant challenges that developers face is the handling of varying data types and formats. As organizations accumulate vast amounts of data from diverse sources, the need for a robust system that can accommodate this heterogeneity becomes paramount. Hadoop, with its distributed architecture, provides a framework that can effectively manage and process different data types, but this capability does not come without its complexities.

Understanding Data Types

Data can be classified into several types, including structured, semi-structured, and unstructured data:

- **Structured Data:** This type of data is organized in a predefined manner, typically in rows and columns, making it easily searchable. Examples include relational databases and spreadsheets.

- **Semi-Structured Data:** This data does not conform to a strict schema but still contains tags or markers to separate data elements. Examples include JSON, XML, and CSV files.

- **Unstructured Data:** This is data that lacks a predefined format or structure, making it challenging to analyze. Examples include text documents, images, videos, and social media posts.

The diversity of data types necessitates a flexible approach to data processing, as each type requires different handling methods.

OVERCOMING TECHNICAL OBSTACLES

Challenges in Data Handling

The primary challenges in managing varying data types and formats include:

- **Data Ingestion:** The process of collecting and importing data from various sources into Hadoop can be complicated by the differences in formats. For instance, a JSON file may require different parsing techniques than a CSV file.

- **Schema Evolution:** As data sources evolve, the schema may change, leading to compatibility issues. For example, adding new fields to a JSON object can create challenges for existing processing jobs that expect a specific structure.

- **Data Quality:** Ensuring data quality becomes more difficult with varying formats, as inconsistencies and errors can arise during data transformation and loading processes.

- **Performance Optimization:** Different data types can affect performance, as certain formats may require more processing power and memory. For example, unstructured data may necessitate additional computational resources for analysis compared to structured data.

Solutions in Hadoop

Hadoop provides several tools and frameworks to address these challenges:

- **Apache Hive:** Hive allows users to query structured data using a SQL-like language. It abstracts the complexity of data formats by providing a schema-on-read capability, enabling users to define the structure of data at the time of querying rather than at the time of storage.

$$\text{SELECT column1, column2 FROM table WHERE condition;} \quad (29)$$

- **Apache Pig:** Pig is a high-level platform for creating programs that run on Hadoop. It offers a scripting language (Pig Latin) that simplifies the process of data manipulation and can handle both structured and semi-structured data formats.

+ **Apache Avro:** Avro is a data serialization system that provides a compact binary format for data storage. It supports schema evolution, allowing users to change the schema without breaking existing data processing jobs.

$$\text{Avro Schema: } \{"type" : "record", "name" : "User", "fields" : ["name" : "name} \tag{30}$$

+ **Apache Spark:** Spark provides an advanced data processing engine capable of handling various data types and formats. It supports in-memory processing, which can significantly improve performance when dealing with unstructured data.

Real-World Examples

To illustrate how Hadoop effectively handles varying data types, consider the following scenarios:

1. **Social Media Analytics:** A company collects data from multiple social media platforms, including text posts, images, and videos. Using Hadoop's ecosystem, they can ingest and process this unstructured data using Spark for real-time analytics, while also leveraging Hive for structured reporting on engagement metrics.

2. **E-Commerce Data Processing:** An e-commerce platform accumulates structured data from transaction logs, semi-structured data from customer reviews (in JSON format), and unstructured data from product images. By employing Avro for data serialization and Hive for querying, the platform can seamlessly analyze customer behavior across different data types.

3. **Healthcare Data Integration:** A healthcare provider integrates data from electronic health records (structured), lab results (semi-structured), and clinical notes (unstructured). Using Pig for data transformation and Spark for analytics, the provider can extract meaningful insights to improve patient care.

Conclusion

Handling varying data types and formats is a critical aspect of big data processing. Hadoop's flexible architecture, along with its suite of tools, empowers organizations to effectively manage diverse datasets. By leveraging the capabilities of Hive, Pig, Avro, and Spark, developers can overcome the challenges associated with data heterogeneity, ensuring that valuable insights can be extracted regardless of the data's origin or format. As the landscape of data continues to evolve, mastering these techniques will be essential for any data professional aiming to thrive in the age of big data.

Security and Privacy Concerns

In the realm of big data, security and privacy are paramount concerns that have evolved alongside the technologies designed to manage and analyze vast amounts of information. As Hadoop emerged as a powerful framework for processing large datasets, it also faced significant scrutiny regarding how it handled sensitive information. This section delves into the theoretical underpinnings of security and privacy in data processing, the inherent problems associated with these challenges, and relevant examples that illustrate the complexities involved.

Theoretical Foundations

At its core, data security refers to the measures taken to protect digital information from unauthorized access, corruption, or theft throughout its lifecycle. Privacy, on the other hand, encompasses the rights and expectations of individuals regarding their personal information. The intersection of these two concepts is critical in the context of Hadoop, which operates on distributed systems where data is often stored across multiple nodes.

The fundamental principles of data security can be summarized by the CIA triad: Confidentiality, Integrity, and Availability.

- **Confidentiality** ensures that sensitive information is accessed only by authorized individuals. This is particularly challenging in Hadoop's distributed environment, where data may be replicated across various nodes.

- **Integrity** guarantees that data remains accurate and unaltered during processing. In Hadoop, data integrity can be compromised through unauthorized modifications or failures in data replication.

- **Availability** ensures that data is accessible when needed. Hadoop's architecture must account for potential node failures while maintaining continuous access to data.

Challenges in Hadoop

Despite its powerful capabilities, Hadoop presents unique challenges in addressing security and privacy concerns. The architecture of Hadoop, which employs a master-slave model with the Hadoop Distributed File System (HDFS), introduces several vulnerabilities:

1. **Data Exposure:** Data stored in HDFS can be exposed to unauthorized users if proper access controls are not implemented. The default configuration may allow broad access, leading to potential data breaches.

2. **Insecure Data Transmission:** Hadoop uses various protocols for data transmission between nodes. If these communications are not encrypted, sensitive data may be intercepted during transit.

3. **Lack of Auditing:** Many Hadoop implementations lack comprehensive logging and auditing capabilities, making it difficult to track access and modifications to data.

Regulatory Compliance

As organizations increasingly adopt Hadoop for big data analytics, they must also navigate a landscape of regulatory compliance. Laws such as the General Data Protection Regulation (GDPR) and the Health Insurance Portability and Accountability Act (HIPAA) impose strict guidelines on how personal data is collected, processed, and stored. Non-compliance can result in severe penalties, making it essential for organizations to implement robust security measures within their Hadoop environments.

For instance, GDPR mandates that organizations must obtain explicit consent from individuals before processing their personal data. This requirement necessitates the implementation of mechanisms within Hadoop to ensure that data handling practices align with legal standards.

Examples of Security Measures

To mitigate security and privacy risks, organizations have employed various strategies within their Hadoop ecosystems:

- **Kerberos Authentication:** Hadoop can be configured to use Kerberos, a network authentication protocol that provides strong authentication for client-server applications through secret-key cryptography. This ensures that only authorized users can access Hadoop services.

- **Data Encryption:** Both at-rest and in-transit encryption are crucial for protecting sensitive data. Tools such as Apache Ranger and Apache Sentry can be integrated into Hadoop to enforce fine-grained access control and encryption policies.

- **Auditing and Monitoring:** Implementing auditing tools allows organizations to track access to data and detect any unauthorized attempts. Solutions like Apache Ranger provide auditing capabilities that log user actions and data access patterns.

Conclusion

As Hadoop continues to evolve, addressing security and privacy concerns will remain a critical focus for developers and organizations alike. The balance between leveraging the power of big data and ensuring the protection of sensitive information is delicate and requires ongoing vigilance. By understanding the theoretical foundations of security and privacy, recognizing the inherent challenges, and implementing robust security measures, the Hadoop community can foster a more secure environment for data processing.

Ultimately, the journey of Hadoop in navigating security and privacy concerns reflects a broader narrative in the tech industry, where innovation must be matched with responsibility. As Doug Cutting and his team laid the groundwork for Hadoop, they also paved the way for future discussions on the ethical implications of data processing in an increasingly data-driven world.

Ensuring Data Integrity and Reliability

In the realm of big data, ensuring data integrity and reliability is paramount. As data is generated at unprecedented rates, the challenge of maintaining accurate and consistent information becomes increasingly complex. Doug Cutting, the visionary behind Hadoop, recognized early on that for a data processing framework to be effective, it must prioritize the integrity of the data it handles. This section explores the theoretical underpinnings, challenges, and practical solutions that Hadoop employs to ensure data integrity and reliability.

Theoretical Foundations

Data integrity refers to the accuracy and consistency of data over its lifecycle. It encompasses several key principles, including:

- **Atomicity:** Ensures that a series of operations within a transaction are completed fully or not at all.

- **Consistency:** Guarantees that a transaction will bring the database from one valid state to another, maintaining all predefined rules.

- **Isolation:** Ensures that transactions are securely and independently processed at the same time without interference.

- **Durability:** Guarantees that once a transaction has been committed, it will remain so, even in the event of a system failure.

These principles are foundational to any robust data management system. Hadoop implements these principles through its distributed architecture, designed to handle data across multiple nodes while maintaining high levels of integrity.

Challenges in Data Integrity

Hadoop faces several challenges in maintaining data integrity and reliability:

- **Node Failures:** In a distributed system, individual nodes may fail, leading to potential data loss or corruption.

- **Data Replication:** While Hadoop's HDFS (Hadoop Distributed File System) replicates data across nodes to enhance reliability, this process can lead to inconsistencies if not managed correctly.

- **Concurrent Access:** Multiple users or processes may attempt to access and modify the same data simultaneously, risking data integrity.

- **Data Corruption:** External factors, such as hardware failures or software bugs, can corrupt data stored in the system.

To address these challenges, Hadoop employs various strategies that leverage its architecture and design principles.

Strategies for Ensuring Data Integrity

Data Replication Hadoop's HDFS automatically replicates data blocks across multiple nodes. By default, each block is replicated three times. This redundancy ensures that even if one or two nodes fail, the data remains accessible from other nodes. The replication factor can be adjusted based on the criticality of the data and the available storage resources.

$$R = \frac{N}{D} \qquad (31)$$

OVERCOMING TECHNICAL OBSTACLES

Where R is the replication factor, N is the total number of data blocks, and D is the number of nodes in the cluster. This equation illustrates how replication distributes data across the cluster, enhancing reliability.

Checksums Hadoop employs checksums to verify data integrity. Each data block written to HDFS is accompanied by a checksum, which is calculated using a hashing algorithm. When data is read, Hadoop recalculates the checksum and compares it to the original. If a mismatch occurs, the system can automatically retrieve the data from another replica.

$$C = H(D) \qquad (32)$$

Where C is the checksum, H is the hashing function, and D is the data block. This method ensures that any corruption can be detected and corrected.

Write-Ahead Logging Hadoop's architecture includes a write-ahead logging mechanism. Before any changes are made to the data, they are first written to a log file. This approach ensures that in the event of a failure, the system can recover to a consistent state by replaying the log.

Examples of Data Integrity in Action

One notable example of Hadoop's commitment to data integrity is its use in financial services. In these industries, data accuracy is critical for compliance and operational efficiency. Hadoop's ability to handle vast amounts of transactional data while ensuring accuracy has made it a preferred choice for banks and financial institutions.

Another example can be found in the healthcare sector, where patient data must be both accurate and secure. Hadoop's robust data integrity measures allow healthcare providers to analyze patient records without compromising the quality or reliability of the data.

Conclusion

Ensuring data integrity and reliability is a cornerstone of Hadoop's architecture. Through a combination of replication, checksums, and write-ahead logging, Hadoop addresses the inherent challenges of distributed data processing. Doug Cutting's foresight in implementing these strategies has not only contributed to Hadoop's success but has also set a standard for data integrity in the big data landscape. As data continues to grow in volume and complexity, the principles established by Cutting will remain vital in guiding future innovations in data processing and management.

Performance Optimization

Performance optimization in Hadoop is a critical aspect that directly influences the efficiency and speed of data processing tasks. As organizations began to adopt Hadoop for handling large datasets, it became evident that optimizing performance was essential to leverage its full potential. This section delves into the theoretical foundations, common problems, and practical examples of performance optimization in Hadoop.

Theoretical Foundations of Performance Optimization

At its core, performance optimization in distributed systems like Hadoop revolves around several key principles: data locality, resource allocation, and parallel processing. The goal is to minimize latency and maximize throughput while ensuring efficient resource utilization.

Data Locality Data locality is a fundamental concept in Hadoop that refers to the idea of processing data where it is stored. By moving computation closer to the data, Hadoop reduces the need for data transfer across the network, which can be a significant bottleneck. The principle is mathematically represented as:

$$\text{Latency} = \text{Data Transfer Time} + \text{Processing Time}$$

To optimize performance, Hadoop strives to minimize the data transfer time, thereby reducing overall latency. This is achieved by employing a master-slave architecture where the Hadoop Distributed File System (HDFS) stores data across various nodes, and the computation is executed on the nodes that contain the relevant data.

Resource Allocation Effective resource allocation ensures that tasks are evenly distributed among the available nodes in the cluster. Hadoop utilizes the YARN (Yet Another Resource Negotiator) framework to manage resources dynamically. YARN allows multiple data processing engines to run on a single cluster, optimizing resource usage. The resource allocation problem can be modeled as an optimization problem:

OVERCOMING TECHNICAL OBSTACLES

$$\text{Minimize} \quad \sum_{i=1}^{n} \text{Latency}_i$$

$$\text{Subject to} \quad \sum_{j=1}^{m} \text{Resource}_j \leq \text{Total Resources}$$

Here, n represents the number of tasks, and m represents the number of resources available. The objective is to minimize the total latency while adhering to resource constraints.

Parallel Processing Hadoop's ability to process data in parallel is another significant factor in performance optimization. By dividing large datasets into smaller chunks and processing them simultaneously across multiple nodes, Hadoop can significantly reduce processing time. The speedup achieved through parallel processing can be expressed using Amdahl's Law:

$$S = \frac{1}{(1-P) + \frac{P}{N}}$$

Where: - S is the speedup, - P is the proportion of the program that can be parallelized, - N is the number of processors.

As N increases, the speedup approaches $\frac{1}{(1-P)}$, highlighting the diminishing returns of parallelization when P is not close to 1.

Common Performance Problems in Hadoop

Despite its robust architecture, Hadoop users often encounter performance issues that can hinder data processing tasks. Some of the most common problems include:

Skewed Data Data skew occurs when a disproportionate amount of data is assigned to a single task, causing that task to take significantly longer to complete than others. This can lead to underutilization of resources and increased overall processing time. To mitigate data skew, techniques such as partitioning and salting can be employed.

Inefficient MapReduce Jobs MapReduce jobs can become inefficient if not designed properly. Common pitfalls include excessive shuffling of data between the map and reduce phases, which can lead to increased I/O operations and latency. Optimizing the number of mappers and reducers, as well as minimizing the amount of data shuffled, can significantly enhance performance.

Configuration Issues Hadoop's performance can be heavily influenced by its configuration settings. Parameters such as memory allocation, the number of reducers, and block sizes must be carefully tuned to match the specific workload. Misconfigurations can lead to resource contention and degraded performance.

Examples of Performance Optimization Techniques

To illustrate the concepts discussed, we can explore several practical optimization techniques employed in Hadoop.

Tuning Hadoop Configuration One of the first steps in optimizing performance is tuning Hadoop's configuration settings. For instance, adjusting the 'mapreduce.map.memory.mb' and 'mapreduce.reduce.memory.mb' parameters can help allocate sufficient memory for mappers and reducers, reducing the likelihood of out-of-memory errors and improving task execution speed.

Combiner Functions Using combiner functions can reduce the amount of data shuffled between the map and reduce phases. A combiner acts as a mini-reducer that processes intermediate data on the mapper nodes before sending it to the reducers. This can significantly reduce network traffic and improve performance.

Using Columnar Storage Formats Employing columnar storage formats such as Parquet or ORC can enhance performance by reducing the amount of data read from disk. These formats allow for efficient compression and encoding, which not only saves storage space but also speeds up read operations, especially for analytical queries that only require a subset of columns.

Optimizing Join Operations Join operations can be particularly expensive in Hadoop. To optimize joins, techniques such as broadcast joins (where smaller datasets are sent to all mapper nodes) or partitioned joins (where datasets are partitioned on the join key) can be employed to minimize data movement and reduce processing time.

Conclusion

Performance optimization in Hadoop is a multifaceted challenge that requires a deep understanding of both the theoretical principles and practical techniques involved. By focusing on data locality, efficient resource allocation, and parallel processing, developers can significantly enhance the performance of their Hadoop applications.

Addressing common performance problems and employing optimization techniques can lead to faster data processing, reduced costs, and ultimately, greater success in leveraging big data analytics.

In summary, as Hadoop continues to evolve, the importance of performance optimization remains paramount. By continually refining these strategies, organizations can ensure that they remain at the forefront of the big data revolution, harnessing the power of Hadoop to drive innovation and growth.

Industry Recognition and Awards

Doug Cutting's Accolades

Doug Cutting, a name synonymous with innovation in the world of big data, has received numerous accolades throughout his illustrious career. His contributions to the field of computing, particularly through the development of Hadoop and other open-source projects, have not only revolutionized data processing but also earned him recognition from various esteemed organizations and institutions.

Recognition in the Tech Community

One of the most significant accolades Doug received is the **O'Reilly Open Source Award**, which he was honored with in 2008. This award is given to individuals who have made substantial contributions to the open-source community. Doug's work on Hadoop, Lucene, and Nutch exemplifies the spirit of open-source development, where collaboration and innovation flourish. His ability to create tools that empower developers and organizations alike has cemented his reputation as a leading figure in the tech community.

Awards from Professional Organizations

In addition to the O'Reilly Open Source Award, Doug has been recognized by the **ACM (Association for Computing Machinery)** as a distinguished member. This honor is reserved for those who have made significant contributions to the computing community and reflects Doug's impact on the field. The ACM's recognition highlights his role in shaping modern data processing technologies and his commitment to advancing computing through open-source initiatives.

Academic Honors

Doug's influence extends beyond the corporate world into academia, where he has been invited to speak at numerous conferences and universities. In 2014, he was awarded an honorary doctorate from **University of California, Berkeley**, acknowledging his contributions to computer science and the impact of his work on the academic landscape. This honor signifies not just recognition of his technical achievements but also his role in inspiring future generations of computer scientists and engineers.

Industry Impact Awards

The impact of Hadoop on the tech industry has also been recognized through various awards. For instance, in 2013, Hadoop was named one of the **Top 10 Technologies** by *InfoWorld*, underscoring its transformative effect on data storage and processing. Doug Cutting, as the co-creator, was acknowledged for his pivotal role in the development of this groundbreaking framework. Such recognition emphasizes the importance of Hadoop in the evolution of big data technologies.

Lifetime Achievement Awards

In 2021, Doug was honored with the **Lifetime Achievement Award** at the *Data Science Summit*. This prestigious award celebrates individuals who have made a lasting impact on the field of data science. Doug's vision and relentless pursuit of innovation in data processing have not only changed the way organizations handle data but have also set the stage for future advancements in the field.

Conclusion

Doug Cutting's accolades are a testament to his brilliance and dedication to the field of computing. His journey, marked by innovation and collaboration, has inspired countless individuals in the tech community. Through his accolades, we see the recognition of a visionary who has not only contributed to the evolution of technology but has also paved the way for future innovations in data processing. As we reflect on his achievements, it is clear that Doug Cutting's legacy will continue to influence the landscape of computing for years to come.

Hadoop's Influence on the Tech Industry

Hadoop, since its inception, has dramatically transformed the tech industry, particularly in the realm of data processing and analytics. This open-source framework, designed to facilitate the distributed processing of large data sets across clusters of computers, has not only changed how companies handle data but has also influenced the development of numerous technologies and methodologies that have become standards in the industry.

The Shift to Big Data

One of the most significant impacts of Hadoop has been its role in the emergence of the "big data" phenomenon. Prior to Hadoop, traditional data processing systems struggled to manage the volume, velocity, and variety of data generated in the digital age. With the advent of Hadoop, organizations could process vast amounts of unstructured and semi-structured data efficiently. This shift has led to a paradigm where data is viewed as a critical asset, driving decision-making processes across various sectors, including finance, healthcare, retail, and technology.

The concept of big data can be encapsulated by the three Vs: Volume, Velocity, and Variety. Hadoop's architecture is particularly well-suited to address these challenges:

- **Volume:** Hadoop can store and process petabytes of data, enabling organizations to harness vast data repositories.

- **Velocity:** With its ability to handle real-time data streams, Hadoop allows for timely analytics and insights.

- **Variety:** Hadoop supports various data types, from structured databases to unstructured text, images, and videos.

Ecosystem Development

Hadoop's influence extends beyond its core framework; it has catalyzed the development of a rich ecosystem of tools and technologies. Projects such as Apache Hive, Apache Pig, and Apache HBase have emerged as essential components of the Hadoop ecosystem, providing additional functionalities for data querying, processing, and storage. For instance, Hive enables SQL-like querying of data stored in Hadoop, making it accessible to analysts and data scientists familiar with relational databases.

The integration of these tools has led to the establishment of a comprehensive data processing ecosystem that empowers organizations to derive insights from their data more effectively. Furthermore, the rise of cloud computing has seen

Hadoop adapted for cloud-based solutions, enhancing its accessibility and scalability. Companies like Amazon Web Services (AWS) and Google Cloud Platform (GCP) have integrated Hadoop into their offerings, making it easier for businesses to leverage big data without the need for extensive on-premises infrastructure.

Driving Innovation in Analytics

Hadoop has also been a driving force behind innovations in data analytics. The ability to process large data sets has paved the way for advanced analytics techniques, including machine learning and artificial intelligence. Organizations can now analyze customer behavior, predict trends, and optimize operations using predictive analytics, all made possible by the capabilities of Hadoop.

For example, retail giants like Walmart and Target utilize Hadoop to analyze consumer purchasing patterns, enabling them to tailor marketing strategies and improve inventory management. Similarly, in the healthcare sector, institutions leverage Hadoop to analyze patient data, leading to improved patient outcomes and operational efficiencies.

Changing the Business Landscape

The influence of Hadoop on the tech industry has led to a shift in the business landscape. Companies that have embraced Hadoop and big data analytics have gained a competitive edge, while those that have not faced the risk of obsolescence. This has prompted a cultural shift within organizations, where data-driven decision-making has become the norm rather than the exception.

Moreover, Hadoop has democratized access to data analytics, allowing smaller companies and startups to compete with larger enterprises. The open-source nature of Hadoop has reduced the barriers to entry for organizations looking to leverage big data, enabling innovation and entrepreneurship in the tech industry.

Conclusion

In conclusion, Hadoop's influence on the tech industry is profound and multifaceted. It has redefined how organizations approach data, catalyzed the development of a robust ecosystem of tools, driven innovation in analytics, and transformed the business landscape. As we look to the future, the legacy of Hadoop will continue to shape the evolution of data processing, ensuring that organizations remain agile and competitive in an increasingly data-driven world.

Impact on Data Science and Analytics

The advent of Hadoop has significantly transformed the landscape of data science and analytics, providing a robust framework for processing vast amounts of data efficiently. Before Hadoop, traditional data processing systems struggled to handle the exponential growth of data generated by various sources, including social media, IoT devices, and online transactions. As a result, data scientists faced numerous challenges in extracting meaningful insights from this deluge of information.

One of the primary contributions of Hadoop to data science is its ability to manage and process unstructured and semi-structured data. Traditional relational databases typically require data to be structured in a predefined schema, which limits their flexibility. In contrast, Hadoop's distributed file system (HDFS) allows for the storage of data in its raw form, enabling data scientists to analyze diverse datasets without the need for extensive preprocessing. This capability is particularly valuable when dealing with data from sources like social media, where formats can vary widely.

$$\text{Total Data Processed} = \sum_{i=1}^{n} \text{Data}_i \tag{33}$$

In this equation, Data_i represents individual data points from various sources, and n is the total number of data points. Hadoop's architecture allows for parallel processing of these data points, which significantly speeds up the analysis process.

Furthermore, Hadoop's ecosystem includes various tools and frameworks that enhance its capabilities in data science. For instance, Apache Pig and Apache Hive provide high-level abstractions for data manipulation and querying, making it easier for data scientists to write complex data transformations and analyses without needing to delve into lower-level programming. This democratization of data processing empowers more professionals to engage in data science, as it lowers the barrier to entry.

A notable example of Hadoop's impact on data science is its application in predictive analytics. Organizations across industries leverage Hadoop to build predictive models that analyze historical data and forecast future trends. For instance, retail companies utilize Hadoop to analyze customer purchase history, enabling them to predict future buying behaviors and optimize inventory management. This predictive capability not only enhances operational efficiency but also improves customer satisfaction by ensuring that products are available when needed.

Moreover, Hadoop has facilitated the rise of machine learning in data science. With the integration of frameworks like Apache Mahout and Spark MLlib, data scientists can implement machine learning algorithms on large datasets efficiently. These tools allow for the training of models that can identify patterns and make predictions based on data. For example, a financial institution may use Hadoop to analyze transaction data and build a fraud detection model that flags suspicious activities in real time.

$$\text{Model Accuracy} = \frac{\text{True Positives} + \text{True Negatives}}{\text{Total Predictions}} \quad (34)$$

In this equation, model accuracy is a critical metric for evaluating the performance of machine learning models. Hadoop's ability to process large volumes of data enables data scientists to train models on comprehensive datasets, leading to improved accuracy and reliability in predictions.

Despite its advantages, the integration of Hadoop into data science is not without challenges. Data scientists must still contend with issues related to data quality and governance. The sheer volume of data processed by Hadoop can lead to inconsistencies and inaccuracies if not managed properly. Therefore, establishing robust data governance frameworks is essential to ensure that the insights derived from Hadoop are trustworthy and actionable.

In conclusion, the impact of Hadoop on data science and analytics is profound and multifaceted. By providing a scalable, flexible, and powerful platform for data processing, Hadoop has enabled organizations to harness the full potential of their data. From predictive analytics to machine learning, the applications of Hadoop in data science continue to evolve, shaping the future of how insights are generated and utilized across various sectors. As data continues to grow in volume and complexity, Hadoop will remain a cornerstone of data science, driving innovation and discovery in the field.

Hadoop in Academia and Research

Hadoop has not only transformed the tech industry but has also made significant strides in academia and research. The framework's ability to process vast amounts of data efficiently has led to its adoption in various educational institutions and research organizations. In this section, we explore the role of Hadoop in academic settings, its influence on research methodologies, and its contribution to the development of data science as a discipline.

Integration into Academic Curricula

The emergence of big data has necessitated the inclusion of data processing technologies in academic curricula. Many universities have integrated Hadoop into their computer science and data science programs. Courses focusing on big data analytics, data mining, and distributed computing now often feature Hadoop as a core component. For instance, institutions like Stanford University and MIT offer specialized courses that delve into the architecture and applications of Hadoop, equipping students with the skills needed to navigate the complexities of big data.

Students engage in hands-on projects using Hadoop, allowing them to apply theoretical knowledge in practical scenarios. This experiential learning approach fosters a deeper understanding of data processing and prepares students for careers in data science, analytics, and related fields.

Research Applications

Hadoop's ability to handle large datasets makes it an invaluable tool for researchers across various domains. In fields such as genomics, social sciences, and climate research, Hadoop has been employed to analyze massive amounts of data that were previously unmanageable.

For example, in genomics, researchers utilize Hadoop to process genomic sequences and identify patterns related to diseases. The ability to store and analyze terabytes of data in a distributed manner has accelerated discoveries in personalized medicine and genetic research.

In social sciences, Hadoop facilitates the analysis of social media data, enabling researchers to gain insights into public sentiment, trends, and behaviors. By harnessing the power of Hadoop, academics can conduct large-scale studies that were once thought impractical.

Collaborative Research Initiatives

Hadoop has also fostered collaboration among researchers, allowing for the sharing of data and resources. Initiatives such as the Apache Software Foundation's commitment to open-source development encourage researchers to contribute to and benefit from the collective knowledge of the community.

Collaborative projects often involve partnerships between universities and industry leaders, where Hadoop is employed to tackle real-world problems. For instance, the collaboration between universities and healthcare organizations has led to innovative solutions for managing patient data and improving healthcare delivery through data analytics.

Challenges in Academia

Despite its advantages, the integration of Hadoop in academia is not without challenges. One significant barrier is the steep learning curve associated with distributed computing frameworks. Students and researchers may struggle to grasp the complexities of Hadoop's architecture, which can hinder its adoption in academic settings.

Moreover, the rapid evolution of technology poses another challenge. Keeping curricula up-to-date with the latest advancements in Hadoop and big data technologies requires continuous effort from educational institutions. Faculty members must engage in ongoing professional development to stay abreast of new features and best practices.

Future Prospects

Looking ahead, the role of Hadoop in academia and research is poised to grow. As the demand for data-driven decision-making increases, educational institutions will continue to emphasize the importance of big data technologies in their programs.

Research initiatives leveraging Hadoop will likely expand, leading to breakthroughs in various fields. The framework's scalability and flexibility make it an ideal candidate for addressing the growing data challenges faced by researchers.

In conclusion, Hadoop's influence in academia and research is profound. By integrating Hadoop into curricula, facilitating large-scale research projects, and fostering collaboration, educational institutions are preparing the next generation of data scientists and researchers. As Hadoop continues to evolve, its role in academia will undoubtedly expand, shaping the future of data processing and analysis.

$$\text{Data Processing Time} = \frac{\text{Total Data Size}}{\text{Processing Speed}} \tag{35}$$

This equation highlights the efficiency of Hadoop in processing large datasets, where increasing the processing speed through distributed computing can significantly reduce the overall data processing time. This efficiency is crucial for researchers who rely on timely analysis to inform their studies.

Legacy and Future of Hadoop

Hadoop, the open-source framework for distributed storage and processing of large data sets, has left an indelible mark on the tech landscape since its inception. As we delve into the legacy and future of Hadoop, it is essential to recognize both the theoretical foundations that underpin its architecture and the practical implications it has had on data processing in various industries.

Hadoop's Legacy

The legacy of Hadoop can be understood through several key dimensions: its architectural innovations, its role in the rise of big data, and its influence on subsequent technologies.

Architectural Innovations   At the core of Hadoop's architecture lies the Hadoop Distributed File System (HDFS) and the MapReduce programming model. HDFS allows for the storage of vast amounts of data across multiple machines, ensuring fault tolerance and high availability. The MapReduce model provides a programming paradigm that enables the processing of large data sets in parallel, significantly improving computational efficiency. The theoretical underpinnings of these components can be expressed through the following equations:

$$\text{Total Data Processed} = \sum_{i=1}^{n} \text{Data}_i \qquad (36)$$

where n is the number of data nodes in the cluster. This equation illustrates how Hadoop scales horizontally, allowing for the addition of more nodes to handle increased data volumes.

Rise of Big Data   Hadoop played a pivotal role in the emergence of the big data phenomenon. As organizations began to collect and analyze massive amounts of data, Hadoop provided the necessary tools to store, manage, and derive insights from this data. The ability to process unstructured data in various formats—such as text, images, and videos—has transformed industries ranging from finance to healthcare.

For instance, companies like Yahoo! and Facebook leveraged Hadoop to analyze user interactions, leading to improved user experiences and targeted advertising. This shift in data handling is encapsulated in the following theoretical framework:

$$\text{Value from Data} = f(\text{Data Quality}, \text{Data Volume}, \text{Data Variety}) \qquad (37)$$

This function highlights how the interplay of quality, volume, and variety of data contributes to the overall value derived from data analytics.

Future of Hadoop

As we look ahead, the future of Hadoop remains vibrant, yet it is also marked by challenges and competition from emerging technologies. The evolution of data processing frameworks, such as Apache Spark and cloud-based solutions, poses questions about Hadoop's relevance in an ever-changing landscape.

Integration with Emerging Technologies Hadoop's future will be significantly influenced by its ability to integrate with new technologies. For example, the rise of machine learning and artificial intelligence necessitates advanced data processing capabilities. Hadoop's ecosystem is adapting to these needs through projects like Apache Mahout and Apache Spark, which enhance its analytical capabilities.

The theoretical implications of this integration can be summarized by the following equation, which represents the synergy between Hadoop and machine learning frameworks:

$$\text{Enhanced Insights} = \text{Hadoop} + \text{Machine Learning} \tag{38}$$

This equation signifies that the combination of Hadoop's robust data processing capabilities with machine learning algorithms can yield deeper insights and more accurate predictions.

Challenges and Competition Despite its strengths, Hadoop faces challenges that could impact its future. The increasing demand for real-time data processing and the need for simplified data management solutions have led to the rise of alternatives that offer faster, more user-friendly experiences. For instance, cloud-native solutions like Google BigQuery and Amazon Redshift provide scalable data warehousing capabilities that can outperform traditional Hadoop clusters in certain scenarios.

Moreover, the complexity of managing a Hadoop ecosystem can deter organizations from adopting it. The need for skilled personnel to manage and optimize Hadoop clusters adds another layer of difficulty. To address these challenges, the Hadoop community must focus on enhancing usability, streamlining deployment processes, and providing comprehensive support for users.

Conclusion

In conclusion, Hadoop's legacy is characterized by its groundbreaking contributions to data storage and processing, its role in the big data revolution, and its ongoing evolution in response to emerging technologies. As we move forward, the future of Hadoop will depend on its ability to adapt to changing demands and integrate with new frameworks while maintaining its core strengths. The journey of Hadoop is far from over; it continues to shape the landscape of data processing and will undoubtedly influence the next generation of technologies that emerge in this dynamic field.

The Man Behind the Code

Doug Cutting's Personality and Character

Early Influences and Values

Doug Cutting's journey into the world of programming and technology was significantly shaped by his early influences and values, which laid the foundation for his remarkable career. Growing up in a family that valued education and intellectual curiosity, Doug was exposed to a myriad of ideas and concepts from a young age. His parents, both educators, instilled in him the importance of learning and the pursuit of knowledge, which would become a guiding principle throughout his life.

One of the most profound influences on Doug was his father, who was a professor of mathematics. The mathematical rigor and logical thinking that Doug observed in his father's work sparked an early interest in problem-solving and analytical thinking. Mathematics, often referred to as the language of the universe, played a crucial role in shaping Doug's approach to programming. The foundational principles of mathematics, including set theory and algorithms, became integral to his understanding of computer science.

$$\text{Logic} = \text{Mathematics} + \text{Reasoning} \tag{39}$$

This equation symbolizes the synergy between mathematical principles and logical reasoning that Doug embraced. The ability to break down complex problems into manageable components is a skill that is highly valued in programming and software development.

In addition to his father's influence, Doug was also inspired by the burgeoning field of computing during his formative years. The late 1970s and early 1980s marked a significant period in the history of computing, with the introduction of personal computers and programming languages such as BASIC. Doug's fascination with technology was further fueled by the availability of early computer systems, which allowed him to experiment and explore the world of programming firsthand.

His early programming projects, including simple games and applications, were not just about learning to code; they were a means of expressing creativity and innovation. Doug's experiences in creating these projects reinforced the value of perseverance and the importance of learning from failure. Each bug he encountered was not merely a setback but an opportunity to deepen his understanding of programming concepts.

The open-source movement, which gained momentum in the 1990s, also played a pivotal role in shaping Doug's values. The ethos of collaboration, transparency, and community-driven development resonated with him deeply. He recognized that technology could be a powerful tool for democratizing access to information and fostering innovation. This belief would later manifest in his contributions to projects like Hadoop and Lucene, where he championed the principles of open-source software.

Doug's commitment to open-source principles can be encapsulated in the following equation:

$$\text{Innovation} = \text{Collaboration} + \text{Transparency} \qquad (40)$$

This equation highlights the interconnectedness of collaboration and transparency in driving technological advancements. Doug understood that by sharing knowledge and resources, the tech community could collectively tackle complex challenges and create solutions that benefit society as a whole.

Moreover, Doug's values were deeply rooted in a sense of responsibility toward the community. He believed that technology should serve the greater good, and this belief guided his decisions throughout his career. His philanthropic efforts, particularly in education and technology accessibility, reflect his commitment to empowering others through knowledge and innovation.

In summary, Doug Cutting's early influences and values were shaped by a combination of familial guidance, exposure to the evolving field of computing, and a commitment to open-source principles. These elements not only fueled his passion for programming but also laid the groundwork for his future contributions to the tech industry. As he navigated the challenges and successes of his career, these foundational influences remained a constant source of inspiration, guiding him toward a vision of technology that is inclusive, collaborative, and transformative.

The intersection of these influences can be visualized as follows:

This diagram illustrates the multifaceted nature of Doug's early influences and values, showcasing how they converged to shape his identity as a programmer and innovator. Each influence played a critical role in molding his perspective on technology and its potential to effect positive change in the world.

Work Ethic and Problem-Solving Approach

Doug Cutting's work ethic and problem-solving approach have been pivotal in shaping his career and the technologies he has developed. Known for his relentless pursuit of excellence and innovation, Doug embodies the qualities of a true visionary in the tech industry. His work ethic is characterized by dedication, perseverance, and a commitment to open-source principles, which have influenced countless programmers and developers globally.

Dedication to Craft

Doug's dedication to his craft can be traced back to his early years, where he demonstrated an insatiable curiosity and passion for technology. This dedication is not merely a product of hard work; it is a deep-seated belief in the potential of technology to solve real-world problems. For instance, while developing Hadoop, Doug recognized the limitations of existing data processing frameworks. Instead of accepting these limitations, he dedicated himself to creating a solution that was not only effective but also scalable.

Perseverance in the Face of Challenges

One of the hallmarks of Doug's problem-solving approach is his perseverance. Throughout his career, he has faced numerous technical challenges, from scaling Hadoop to accommodate massive datasets to addressing security vulnerabilities. Each obstacle has been met with a steadfast resolve to find a solution.

For example, when Hadoop was initially developed, one of the significant challenges was managing the sheer volume of data generated by modern applications. Doug and his team had to innovate continuously, leading to the development of features such as the Hadoop Distributed File System (HDFS), which allowed for efficient storage and retrieval of large datasets. The formula for efficiency in data processing can be expressed as:

$$E = \frac{D}{T}$$

where E represents efficiency, D is the amount of data processed, and T is the time taken to process that data. Doug's focus on increasing D while minimizing T has driven many of Hadoop's innovations.

Collaborative Problem Solving

Doug's approach to problem-solving is not just individualistic; it is deeply collaborative. He has always believed that the best solutions come from diverse perspectives and collective effort. This belief is reflected in his active participation in the open-source community, where he has encouraged collaboration among developers worldwide.

For example, when developing Lucene, a search engine library, Doug invited contributions from various developers, fostering an environment where ideas could flourish. This collaborative spirit is evident in the way he structured the Hadoop project, encouraging contributions from a wide range of users and developers. The equation that captures the essence of collaborative problem-solving can be represented as:

$$S = \sum_{i=1}^{n} C_i$$

where S is the overall solution, and C_i represents the contributions from individual collaborators. This approach not only enhances the quality of the final product but also builds a robust community around the technology.

Adaptability and Continuous Learning

In the rapidly evolving tech landscape, adaptability is crucial. Doug's ability to learn continuously and adapt to new technologies has been a significant factor in his success. He has often stated that the tech industry is like a moving train; if you don't keep up, you'll be left behind. This mindset has led him to explore new technologies and methodologies, integrating them into his projects.

For instance, the evolution of Hadoop involved incorporating advancements in cloud computing and machine learning. Doug's willingness to embrace these changes has allowed Hadoop to remain relevant and powerful in the face of emerging technologies. The adaptability equation can be expressed as:

$$A = \frac{L}{T}$$

where A is adaptability, L is the learning acquired, and T is the time taken to implement that learning. Doug's high adaptability score has enabled him to lead projects that are not only innovative but also sustainable.

Conclusion

In summary, Doug Cutting's work ethic and problem-solving approach are characterized by dedication, perseverance, collaboration, adaptability, and a commitment to continuous learning. These qualities have not only propelled his career but have also left an indelible mark on the tech industry. As he continues to innovate and inspire future generations of programmers, Doug's legacy serves as a testament to the power of a strong work ethic and a thoughtful approach to problem-solving in the ever-evolving world of technology.

Leadership and Collaboration Style

Doug Cutting's leadership and collaboration style has been a cornerstone of his success as a pioneer in the tech industry, particularly in the realm of open source software. His approach can be characterized by several key principles that not only foster innovation but also promote a culture of inclusivity and shared purpose among collaborators.

Empowerment and Trust

At the heart of Doug's leadership philosophy is the belief in empowering team members. He understands that innovation thrives in an environment where individuals feel trusted and valued. This empowerment manifests in various ways, from encouraging team members to take ownership of their projects to providing them with the autonomy to explore new ideas. Doug often cites the importance of creating a safe space for experimentation, where failures are seen as learning opportunities rather than setbacks. This approach aligns with the transformational leadership theory, which emphasizes the role of leaders in inspiring and motivating their teams to achieve exceptional outcomes.

Collaborative Problem Solving

Doug's collaboration style is deeply rooted in the principles of open source development. He advocates for a collaborative problem-solving approach, where diverse perspectives are not only welcomed but actively sought. This methodology is evident in the development of Hadoop, where contributions from various developers worldwide enriched the project. Doug employs techniques such as brainstorming sessions and hackathons, which encourage creativity and collective intelligence. According to the theory of collective intelligence, groups can outperform individuals in problem-solving tasks, and Doug's leadership exemplifies this principle.

Communication and Transparency

Effective communication is another hallmark of Doug's leadership. He prioritizes transparency in all aspects of project management, ensuring that team members are informed and engaged. This transparency fosters trust and reduces misunderstandings, which can be detrimental to collaborative efforts. Doug often utilizes tools such as mailing lists and forums to facilitate open discussions, allowing contributors to share insights and feedback freely. The importance of communication in teamwork is supported by Tuckman's stages of group development, which highlight how effective communication can enhance team dynamics at every stage, from forming to performing.

Mentorship and Guidance

Doug Cutting is also known for his mentorship style, where he invests time in guiding emerging talents in the tech community. He believes that nurturing the next generation of programmers is essential for the sustainability of the open source movement. His mentorship goes beyond technical guidance; he emphasizes the importance of soft skills such as collaboration, negotiation, and conflict resolution. This aligns with the situational leadership theory, which posits that effective leaders adapt their style based on the development level of their team members. Doug's ability to recognize when to step back and allow others to lead, versus when to provide direction, showcases his adeptness in this area.

Real-World Examples

One notable example of Doug's leadership in action is during the initial development of Hadoop. Faced with the challenge of processing vast amounts of data, Doug brought together a diverse team of engineers and researchers. By fostering an environment of open collaboration and encouraging input from all members, the team was able to innovate rapidly. The result was a framework that not only addressed the immediate needs of data processing but also laid the groundwork for a robust ecosystem of tools and technologies.

Another example can be seen in Doug's work with the Apache Software Foundation. His commitment to open source principles has inspired countless developers to contribute to projects like Lucene and Nutch. By championing a culture of collaboration, Doug has helped create a vibrant community that thrives on shared knowledge and collective achievement.

Conclusion

In conclusion, Doug Cutting's leadership and collaboration style is a blend of empowerment, open communication, and mentorship. His ability to inspire and engage others has not only driven the success of Hadoop but has also made a lasting impact on the tech industry. As we look to the future of data processing, Doug's approach serves as a guiding light for aspiring leaders in technology, illustrating the profound effects of collaborative innovation and inclusive leadership.

Balancing Work and Personal Life

In the fast-paced world of technology, where innovation often demands relentless dedication, the ability to balance work and personal life can be a formidable challenge. Doug Cutting, the visionary behind Hadoop, exemplifies a successful equilibrium between his professional responsibilities and personal pursuits. This balance is not merely a matter of time management; it encompasses a deep understanding of priorities, values, and the importance of well-being.

The Importance of Balance

The significance of maintaining a work-life balance cannot be overstated. Research has shown that a well-rounded life contributes to better mental health, increased productivity, and greater job satisfaction. According to the *American Psychological Association*, individuals who achieve a healthy balance experience lower stress levels and improved overall well-being. In the context of the tech industry, where burnout is prevalent, Doug's approach serves as a beacon for others.

Strategies for Balancing Work and Life

Doug Cutting employs several strategies to maintain this balance:

- **Setting Boundaries:** Establishing clear boundaries between work and home life is crucial. Doug prioritizes his time by designating specific hours for work-related tasks, ensuring that personal time remains uninterrupted.

- **Time Management Techniques:** Utilizing techniques such as the *Pomodoro Technique*, which involves working in focused sprints followed by short breaks, allows Doug to maximize productivity without sacrificing personal time. The formula for the Pomodoro Technique is given by:

$$T_{total} = n \cdot (T_{work} + T_{break})$$

where T_{total} is the total time spent, n is the number of cycles, T_{work} is the duration of focused work, and T_{break} is the duration of rest.

- **Prioritizing Health:** Physical and mental health are paramount. Doug incorporates regular exercise, mindfulness practices, and hobbies into his routine, recognizing that a healthy body and mind enhance his effectiveness at work.

- **Flexible Work Arrangements:** As a proponent of remote work, Doug advocates for flexibility in work arrangements. This adaptability allows him to align his work schedule with personal commitments, fostering a more harmonious life.

- **Quality Time with Family:** Doug places great emphasis on spending quality time with his family. Engaging in family activities not only strengthens relationships but also provides a much-needed respite from work pressures.

Challenges Faced

Despite these strategies, maintaining balance is fraught with challenges. The tech industry is notorious for its demanding schedules and high expectations. Doug has faced moments where the lines between work and personal life blurred, leading to stress and fatigue. Acknowledging these challenges is vital; it allows for proactive adjustments and reinforces the importance of self-care.

Moreover, the advent of technology can sometimes exacerbate the issue. With constant connectivity through emails and messaging apps, the temptation to remain "always on" can lead to a culture of overwork. Doug combats this by consciously unplugging during personal time, understanding that true innovation flourishes when the mind is allowed to rest and rejuvenate.

Examples of Balance in Action

Doug's journey is peppered with examples of how he has successfully navigated the balance between work and personal life. For instance, during the early days of

Hadoop's development, he faced immense pressure to deliver results. However, he made it a point to step back, engage in outdoor activities, and spend weekends with his family. This approach not only kept his creativity flowing but also provided him with fresh perspectives on problem-solving.

Another notable instance occurred when Doug was invited to speak at a major tech conference. Instead of viewing it as an obligation, he seized the opportunity to turn the trip into a family vacation. By integrating work with personal enjoyment, he demonstrated that balance is not just about dividing time but rather about blending experiences.

Conclusion

In conclusion, Doug Cutting's ability to balance work and personal life is a testament to his understanding of the holistic nature of success. By setting boundaries, managing time effectively, prioritizing health, embracing flexibility, and cherishing family moments, he exemplifies a model that many in the tech industry can aspire to. As technology continues to evolve, the importance of maintaining this balance will remain crucial for sustained innovation and personal fulfillment. Doug's journey serves as a reminder that behind every line of code, there lies a life that deserves to be lived fully and joyously.

Philanthropic Contributions

Doug Cutting, recognized primarily for his revolutionary contributions to the field of data processing through Hadoop, has also made significant strides in philanthropy, reflecting his belief in the transformative power of technology and education. His philanthropic efforts are deeply intertwined with his commitment to open source principles, emphasizing accessibility, collaboration, and community empowerment.

Commitment to Education

One of Cutting's primary philanthropic focuses has been on education, particularly in the fields of computer science and technology. He has actively supported various educational initiatives aimed at inspiring the next generation of programmers and technologists. For instance, he has collaborated with organizations such as *Code.org* and *Girls Who Code*, which aim to increase diversity in tech by providing resources and mentorship to underrepresented groups.

$$\text{Educational Impact} = \text{Number of Students} \times \text{Quality of Resources} \quad (41)$$

This equation illustrates how Cutting's contributions can be quantified in terms of educational impact. By increasing both the number of students reached and the quality of resources provided, he aims to foster a more inclusive tech community.

Open Source Advocacy

Cutting's commitment to open source software is another avenue through which he has contributed philanthropically. He has been a strong advocate for the open source movement, believing that technology should be freely accessible to all. By promoting open source projects, he not only enhances technological innovation but also encourages collaboration among developers worldwide.

Through initiatives like the *Apache Software Foundation*, which he helped to elevate, Cutting has ensured that many software projects remain accessible and free for anyone to use, modify, and distribute. This philosophy not only democratizes technology but also empowers individuals and communities to solve their own problems.

Community Engagement

Moreover, Cutting has engaged with local communities through various tech meetups and hackathons. These events serve as platforms for budding developers to collaborate, share ideas, and learn from one another. By facilitating these gatherings, Cutting fosters a spirit of innovation and community that is essential for the growth of the tech ecosystem.

$$\text{Community Growth} = \text{Number of Events} \times \text{Participant Engagement} \quad (42)$$

This equation highlights the importance of both the frequency of events and the level of participant engagement in fostering community growth. Cutting's involvement in these activities has shown that philanthropy in technology is not only about monetary donations but also about nurturing the community.

Global Initiatives

In addition to local efforts, Cutting has supported global initiatives aimed at leveraging technology for social good. He has been involved in projects that utilize big data for humanitarian purposes, such as disaster response and public health monitoring. By applying the principles of data processing to solve pressing global issues, Cutting exemplifies how technology can be a force for good.

For example, during natural disasters, data analytics can play a crucial role in resource allocation and crisis management. By analyzing data from various sources, organizations can make informed decisions that save lives and mitigate damage.

$$\text{Crisis Response Efficiency} = \frac{\text{Resources Allocated}}{\text{Time Taken to Respond}} \quad (43)$$

This equation demonstrates how the efficiency of crisis response can be improved through effective data analysis. Cutting's contributions to projects that focus on such applications illustrate his commitment to using technology for humanitarian purposes.

Legacy of Philanthropy

Ultimately, Doug Cutting's philanthropic contributions extend beyond traditional measures of charity. His focus on education, open source advocacy, community engagement, and global initiatives showcases a holistic approach to giving back. By empowering individuals and communities through technology, he not only enriches lives but also lays the groundwork for a more equitable and innovative future.

As Cutting continues to influence the tech landscape, his philanthropic efforts serve as a reminder that the true measure of success in technology is not just in the innovations created but also in the positive impact made on society. Through his work, he inspires others in the tech community to embrace a similar ethos, fostering a culture of giving that is essential for the sustainable growth of the industry.

In summary, Doug Cutting's philanthropic contributions are a testament to his belief in the power of technology to change lives. By focusing on education, open source advocacy, community engagement, and global initiatives, he has created a legacy that will inspire future generations of technologists to not only innovate but also give back to their communities and the world at large.

The Future of Data Processing

Doug Cutting's Vision for Data Analytics

Doug Cutting, a visionary in the realm of data processing, has consistently emphasized the transformative power of data analytics in understanding complex systems and driving decision-making processes across various domains. His vision is anchored in the belief that data, when harnessed effectively, can unveil insights that were previously obscured, enabling organizations to innovate and operate more efficiently.

At the core of Cutting's philosophy lies the concept of **data democratization**. He advocates for making data accessible to a broader audience, beyond just data scientists and engineers. This democratization is crucial for fostering a culture of data-driven decision-making within organizations. By providing intuitive tools and platforms, Cutting envisions a future where every employee, regardless of their technical background, can leverage data analytics to inform their work. The emergence of user-friendly interfaces and visual analytics tools aligns with this vision, allowing non-technical users to extract insights without needing to understand complex algorithms.

Challenges in Data Analytics

Despite the promising outlook for data analytics, several challenges persist that Doug Cutting has acknowledged in his discussions. One primary issue is the **data silos** that exist within organizations. These silos occur when departments or teams hoard data, leading to fragmentation and inefficiencies. Cutting believes that breaking down these silos is essential for fostering collaboration and ensuring that data can flow freely across the organization.

Another significant challenge is the **quality of data**. Poor data quality can lead to misleading insights and erroneous conclusions. Cutting emphasizes the importance of implementing robust data governance practices to ensure that data is accurate, consistent, and up-to-date. This includes establishing clear protocols for data entry, validation, and maintenance.

Furthermore, Cutting has highlighted the importance of addressing **privacy and security concerns** associated with data analytics. As organizations increasingly rely on data to drive their strategies, they must also prioritize the protection of sensitive information. This involves implementing stringent security measures, such as encryption and access controls, to safeguard data from unauthorized access and breaches.

Theoretical Foundations of Data Analytics

Cutting's vision for data analytics is also grounded in several theoretical frameworks. One such framework is the **CRISP-DM** (Cross-Industry Standard Process for Data Mining) model, which outlines a systematic approach to data mining and analytics projects. This model consists of six phases:

1. **Business Understanding**: Defining project objectives and requirements from a business perspective.

2. **Data Understanding**: Collecting initial data and identifying data quality issues.

3. **Data Preparation**: Preparing the final dataset for modeling, which may involve cleaning and transforming data.

4. **Modeling**: Selecting and applying various modeling techniques to the prepared dataset.

5. **Evaluation**: Assessing the model's performance and ensuring it meets business objectives.

6. **Deployment**: Implementing the model in a production environment for ongoing use.

This structured approach resonates with Cutting's belief in the importance of a systematic methodology for successful data analytics initiatives.

Examples of Data Analytics in Action

Cutting's vision is not merely theoretical; it is exemplified in various real-world applications of data analytics that have transformed industries. For instance, in the healthcare sector, predictive analytics has been utilized to improve patient outcomes by analyzing historical patient data to identify risk factors and predict potential health issues. This proactive approach enables healthcare providers to intervene early, ultimately saving lives and reducing costs.

In the realm of retail, companies like Amazon leverage data analytics to personalize customer experiences. By analyzing purchasing behaviors and preferences, Amazon can recommend products tailored to individual customers, significantly enhancing customer satisfaction and driving sales.

Another notable example is in the field of transportation, where data analytics is employed to optimize logistics and supply chain management. Companies like UPS utilize advanced analytics to streamline delivery routes, reducing fuel consumption and improving delivery times. This not only enhances operational efficiency but also contributes to sustainability efforts.

The Future of Data Analytics

Looking ahead, Doug Cutting envisions a future where advancements in artificial intelligence and machine learning will further revolutionize data analytics. He predicts that as these technologies mature, they will enable even deeper insights and automation of data analysis processes. For instance, automated machine learning (AutoML) tools are emerging that allow users to build predictive models without extensive knowledge of machine learning algorithms. This aligns with Cutting's vision of making data analytics accessible to a wider audience.

Moreover, Cutting anticipates that the integration of **real-time analytics** will become increasingly important. As organizations strive to respond swiftly to changing market conditions, the ability to analyze data in real-time will be a critical competitive advantage. This shift towards real-time analytics will require robust infrastructure and technologies capable of handling vast amounts of data at unprecedented speeds.

In conclusion, Doug Cutting's vision for data analytics is characterized by a commitment to democratization, quality, and security, underpinned by theoretical frameworks and exemplified through practical applications. As the landscape of data analytics continues to evolve, Cutting's insights and contributions will undoubtedly shape the future of how organizations harness the power of data to drive innovation and success.

Current Projects and Ventures

As of late 2023, Doug Cutting remains an influential figure in the tech landscape, actively involved in several projects that continue to shape the future of data processing and analytics. His current endeavors reflect not only his commitment to innovation but also his passion for open-source collaboration and community engagement.

1. Advancements in Apache Hadoop

One of Cutting's primary focuses has been on enhancing the capabilities of Apache Hadoop. With the advent of big data, the need for scalable and efficient data processing frameworks has never been more critical. Cutting has been instrumental in spearheading initiatives aimed at optimizing Hadoop for modern workloads. This includes improvements in the following areas:

- **Performance Enhancements:** Leveraging techniques such as data locality and in-memory processing, the latest iterations of Hadoop have shown

THE FUTURE OF DATA PROCESSING 119

significant performance improvements. For instance, the introduction of the Hadoop `YARN` resource management layer has allowed for more efficient resource allocation and job scheduling, resulting in faster data processing times.

- **Integration with Cloud Technologies:** As organizations increasingly adopt cloud infrastructures, Cutting has advocated for Hadoop's seamless integration with cloud platforms like Amazon Web Services (AWS) and Microsoft Azure. This integration facilitates scalable storage solutions and dynamic resource management, enabling businesses to handle fluctuating data volumes effectively.

- **Enhanced Security Features:** In response to growing concerns around data privacy and security, Cutting has prioritized the development of advanced security protocols within Hadoop, such as `Kerberos` authentication and data encryption methodologies. These features ensure that sensitive data remains protected while being processed in distributed environments.

2. Contributions to Apache NiFi

Another significant venture for Cutting has been his involvement with Apache NiFi, a project designed to automate the flow of data between systems. NiFi's user-friendly interface and robust data routing capabilities have made it a popular choice for organizations looking to streamline their data ingestion processes. Cutting's contributions include:

- **User Experience Improvements:** Recognizing the importance of accessibility, Cutting has worked on enhancing NiFi's graphical user interface (GUI) to make it more intuitive for users. This includes the implementation of drag-and-drop features and real-time monitoring dashboards that provide insights into data flows.

- **Integration with Machine Learning Frameworks:** In an effort to harness the power of machine learning, Cutting has advocated for NiFi's integration with popular ML frameworks like TensorFlow and Apache Spark. This integration allows organizations to preprocess data efficiently before feeding it into machine learning models, thereby improving the overall accuracy and performance of predictive analytics.

3. Promoting Data Literacy

Beyond his technical contributions, Cutting is passionate about promoting data literacy among the next generation of programmers and data scientists. He has initiated several educational programs and workshops aimed at equipping individuals with the necessary skills to thrive in a data-driven world. These initiatives focus on:

- **Hands-on Coding Workshops:** Cutting has organized coding boot camps that emphasize practical experience with open-source tools like Hadoop and NiFi. Participants engage in real-world projects that help them understand the intricacies of data processing and analytics.

- **Mentorship Programs:** Recognizing the importance of mentorship in fostering talent, Cutting has established mentorship networks that connect experienced professionals with aspiring data enthusiasts. These programs provide guidance, resources, and networking opportunities that are invaluable for career development.

4. Future Directions in Data Processing

Looking ahead, Cutting envisions a future where data processing becomes increasingly automated and intelligent. He is exploring the potential of artificial intelligence (AI) and machine learning to enhance data analytics capabilities. Some key areas of focus include:

- **Automated Data Cleaning and Preparation:** One of the most time-consuming aspects of data analysis is the data cleaning process. Cutting is investigating AI-driven solutions that can automatically identify and rectify inconsistencies in datasets, thereby streamlining the analytics pipeline.

- **Real-time Data Processing:** As businesses demand faster insights, Cutting is committed to advancing real-time data processing technologies. By leveraging stream processing frameworks such as Apache Kafka, he aims to enable organizations to make data-driven decisions in near real-time.

- **Ethical AI and Data Usage:** With the growing concern around ethical considerations in AI, Cutting is advocating for frameworks that ensure responsible data usage. This includes promoting transparency in algorithms and fostering discussions around the ethical implications of data collection and analysis.

THE FUTURE OF DATA PROCESSING

In summary, Doug Cutting's current projects and ventures reflect his unwavering commitment to advancing data processing technologies while fostering a culture of collaboration and education. His work not only influences the technical landscape but also inspires the next generation of innovators to harness the power of data responsibly and effectively.

Hadoop's Role in the Future of Computing

Hadoop, an open-source framework that has revolutionized the way we process and store vast amounts of data, is poised to play a significant role in the future of computing. As we delve into the potential that Hadoop holds, it's essential to understand the underlying principles that make it a cornerstone of modern data processing architectures.

The Evolution of Data Processing

The sheer volume of data generated in today's digital landscape is staggering. According to a report by IDC, the global data sphere is expected to reach 175 zettabytes by 2025. This explosion of data necessitates innovative solutions for storage, processing, and analysis. Hadoop's distributed computing model allows organizations to leverage commodity hardware to process large datasets efficiently, making it a critical player in the evolution of data processing.

$$T = \frac{D}{N} \qquad (44)$$

Where:

- T is the time required to process the data,
- D is the total size of the dataset,
- N is the number of nodes in the Hadoop cluster.

This equation illustrates how Hadoop's architecture enables linear scalability, allowing organizations to add more nodes to handle increasing data loads without a corresponding increase in processing time.

Addressing Emerging Challenges

As we look to the future, several challenges must be addressed to harness the full potential of Hadoop. These include:

- **Data Variety:** With the rise of IoT devices, social media, and unstructured data, the ability to process diverse data types is crucial. Hadoop's ecosystem, particularly tools like Apache Spark and Apache Flink, is evolving to support real-time processing and complex event processing, enabling organizations to derive insights from varied data sources.

- **Data Security:** As data breaches become more common, ensuring data security is paramount. Hadoop has made strides in this area with features like Kerberos authentication and integration with Apache Ranger for fine-grained access control. Future developments will likely focus on enhancing encryption methods and compliance with regulations like GDPR.

- **Performance Optimization:** As datasets grow, the need for performance optimization becomes critical. Techniques such as data partitioning, indexing, and the use of in-memory processing frameworks like Apache Spark are essential for achieving faster query times and more efficient resource utilization.

Hadoop in the Cloud Era

The future of computing is increasingly cloud-centric, and Hadoop is adapting to this shift. Cloud platforms like Amazon Web Services (AWS), Microsoft Azure, and Google Cloud Platform (GCP) offer Hadoop as a service, allowing organizations to deploy and scale their Hadoop clusters without the burden of managing physical infrastructure.

$$C = \sum_{i=1}^{n}(P_i \cdot U_i) \qquad (45)$$

Where:

- C is the total cost of running Hadoop in the cloud,
- P_i is the price of each cloud resource,
- U_i is the utilization of each resource.

This equation underscores the cost-effectiveness of cloud-based Hadoop solutions, where organizations can optimize their resource utilization to minimize costs while maximizing performance.

The Integration of AI and Machine Learning

As artificial intelligence (AI) and machine learning (ML) continue to advance, Hadoop's role will increasingly intersect with these technologies. With its ability to handle large datasets, Hadoop serves as an ideal foundation for training machine learning models. Frameworks like Apache Mahout and Apache Spark MLlib provide libraries for building scalable machine learning algorithms on Hadoop.

For example, a retail company can utilize Hadoop to analyze customer purchasing behavior and then apply machine learning algorithms to predict future purchases. The ability to process massive datasets quickly allows for more accurate predictions and personalized marketing strategies.

Future Directions and Innovations

Looking ahead, several innovations are expected to shape Hadoop's future:

- **Serverless Architectures:** The emergence of serverless computing will allow developers to focus on writing code without worrying about the underlying infrastructure. This paradigm shift could lead to more efficient data processing workflows within the Hadoop ecosystem.

- **Enhanced Data Governance:** As organizations grapple with data privacy and compliance issues, Hadoop will need to evolve to offer more robust data governance features. This includes improved metadata management and lineage tracking to ensure data integrity and compliance.

- **Collaboration with Other Technologies:** The future of computing will be characterized by interoperability between different technologies. Hadoop is likely to collaborate more closely with databases, data lakes, and other big data technologies to create a seamless data processing environment.

Conclusion

In conclusion, Hadoop's role in the future of computing is not just as a tool for processing large datasets but as a foundational technology that will enable organizations to navigate the complexities of the data-driven world. As challenges arise and new technologies emerge, Hadoop will continue to adapt and evolve, solidifying its position as a cornerstone of modern data processing architectures. The journey ahead is filled with potential, and with innovators like Doug Cutting at the helm, the future looks promising for Hadoop and the broader computing landscape.

Shaping the Next Generation of Programmers

In the ever-evolving landscape of technology, the influence of seasoned programmers like Doug Cutting extends far beyond their immediate contributions. As a pioneer of big data technologies, Cutting's work has not only revolutionized data processing but has also set a precedent for the next generation of programmers. This subsection explores how Doug Cutting's vision and methodologies are shaping the future of programming, fostering innovation, and inspiring aspiring developers.

Emphasizing Open Source Collaboration

One of the cornerstones of Doug Cutting's philosophy is the belief in the power of open source collaboration. By promoting transparency and collective problem-solving, Cutting has demonstrated that significant advancements can arise from community-driven efforts. The Apache Hadoop project itself serves as a prime example of this ethos.

The open-source model encourages programmers to contribute their ideas and code, leading to a more diverse range of solutions. For instance, the inclusion of various contributors in the Hadoop ecosystem has resulted in innovative tools like Apache Spark and Apache Hive, which extend Hadoop's capabilities.

This collaborative spirit is essential for nurturing the next generation of programmers, as it teaches them the value of teamwork and the importance of sharing knowledge. Aspiring developers are encouraged to engage with open-source projects, contributing their skills while learning from the experiences of others.

Fostering a Growth Mindset

Doug Cutting exemplifies a growth mindset, a concept popularized by psychologist Carol Dweck. This mindset emphasizes the belief that abilities can be developed through dedication and hard work. By embodying this philosophy, Cutting inspires young programmers to embrace challenges and view failures as opportunities for learning.

For example, when faced with the scalability issues of Hadoop in its early days, Cutting and his team did not shy away from the problem. Instead, they approached it with curiosity, iterating on their designs and learning from each setback. This approach not only led to the successful scaling of Hadoop but also instilled resilience in those involved in the project.

Encouraging a growth mindset among new programmers fosters an environment where experimentation and innovation thrive. By promoting this attitude, Cutting influences the next generation to tackle complex problems with confidence and creativity.

Incorporating Real-World Problem Solving

Cutting's work emphasizes the importance of solving real-world problems through programming. His approach to data processing was driven by the need to handle vast amounts of information efficiently, a challenge that many organizations face today.

To inspire the next generation, it is essential to connect programming education with practical applications. For instance, incorporating projects that involve analyzing large datasets or building scalable applications in educational curricula can provide students with hands-on experience.

Consider the example of a student project that involves creating a data analysis tool for a local nonprofit organization. By addressing a tangible problem, students not only apply their programming skills but also understand the impact of their work on the community. This real-world connection is vital for motivating young programmers and demonstrating the significance of their contributions.

Encouraging Ethical Considerations in Technology

As technology continues to permeate every aspect of society, ethical considerations become increasingly important. Doug Cutting's journey highlights the need for responsible programming practices, particularly in the realm of data privacy and security.

The development of Hadoop came with its own set of challenges regarding data integrity and user privacy. By prioritizing these aspects, Cutting sets an example for future programmers to follow.

Incorporating ethics into programming education ensures that the next generation is equipped to make responsible decisions in their work. For example, discussions around data ethics could be integrated into programming courses, encouraging students to consider the implications of their code on individuals and society as a whole.

Mentorship and Community Engagement

Finally, Doug Cutting's commitment to mentorship plays a crucial role in shaping the next generation of programmers. By sharing his knowledge and experiences, he empowers young developers to navigate the complexities of the tech industry.

Engaging with local coding boot camps, universities, and online programming communities allows seasoned programmers to provide guidance and support. For instance, Cutting's participation in workshops and conferences fosters an environment where emerging talent can learn from industry leaders.

Mentorship not only helps young programmers develop technical skills but also instills confidence and a sense of belonging within the tech community. This support system is vital for encouraging diversity and inclusion in programming, ensuring that a wide range of voices contribute to the future of technology.

Conclusion

In conclusion, Doug Cutting's influence on the next generation of programmers is profound and multifaceted. By advocating for open source collaboration, fostering a growth mindset, incorporating real-world problem solving, emphasizing ethical considerations, and engaging in mentorship, Cutting is shaping the future of programming in meaningful ways.

As aspiring developers look to the future, they carry with them the lessons learned from pioneers like Doug Cutting, ensuring that the legacy of innovation, collaboration, and responsibility continues to thrive in the ever-evolving world of technology.

Predictions for Data Processing

As we look toward the future of data processing, it becomes imperative to analyze the trends, challenges, and innovations that will shape the landscape. Doug Cutting's visionary approach to data analytics serves as a guiding light, illuminating potential pathways for the evolution of this field. Below, we explore several key predictions regarding the future of data processing, considering technological advancements, theoretical frameworks, and real-world applications.

1. The Rise of Real-Time Data Processing

With the exponential growth of data generated every second, the demand for real-time data processing is becoming increasingly critical. According to the International Data Corporation (IDC), the amount of data created globally is projected to reach 175 zettabytes by 2025. This surge necessitates the development of systems capable of processing data in real-time, allowing organizations to make timely decisions based on the most current information available.

$$D_{total} = D_{current} + D_{new} \cdot t \tag{46}$$

THE FUTURE OF DATA PROCESSING

Where D_{total} is the total data volume, $D_{current}$ is the existing data volume, D_{new} is the rate of new data generation, and t is time. As real-time systems evolve, we can expect frameworks like Apache Kafka and Apache Flink to gain traction, enabling organizations to harness streaming data effectively.

2. Enhanced Machine Learning Integration

The integration of machine learning (ML) with data processing frameworks is poised to revolutionize the way organizations analyze and leverage their data. As algorithms become more sophisticated, the need for scalable data processing platforms that can handle vast datasets will be paramount. Doug Cutting has emphasized the importance of making machine learning accessible to a broader audience, and we can anticipate a future where user-friendly interfaces and automated ML processes become standard.

The equation below illustrates the relationship between data volume, model complexity, and performance:

$$P = f(V, C) \qquad (47)$$

Where P is the performance of the ML model, V is the volume of data, and C is the complexity of the model. As data volume increases, performance can be optimized through advanced algorithms and distributed processing techniques.

3. Data Privacy and Ethical Considerations

As data processing becomes more pervasive, ethical considerations surrounding data privacy will take center stage. The implementation of regulations like the General Data Protection Regulation (GDPR) and the California Consumer Privacy Act (CCPA) has already begun to shape how organizations collect, store, and process data. Future data processing frameworks will need to incorporate privacy-preserving techniques, such as differential privacy and federated learning, to ensure compliance and maintain user trust.

The challenge of balancing data utility and privacy can be represented as follows:

$$U = \frac{D}{P} \qquad (48)$$

Where U is the utility of the data, D is the data available for processing, and P is the privacy risk. Striking the right balance will be crucial in fostering innovation while safeguarding individual rights.

4. Quantum Computing's Impact on Data Processing

Quantum computing holds the potential to dramatically transform data processing capabilities. By leveraging the principles of quantum mechanics, quantum computers can perform calculations at speeds unattainable by classical computers. This advancement could revolutionize fields such as cryptography, optimization, and complex simulations, enabling organizations to tackle problems previously deemed infeasible.

The potential speedup of quantum algorithms can be illustrated by Grover's search algorithm, which offers a quadratic speedup for unstructured search problems:

$$T_{quantum} = \frac{T_{classical}}{\sqrt{N}} \qquad (49)$$

Where $T_{quantum}$ is the time taken by a quantum algorithm, $T_{classical}$ is the time taken by a classical algorithm, and N is the number of elements in the dataset. As quantum computing matures, it will undoubtedly influence data processing paradigms.

5. The Evolution of Data Storage Solutions

The future of data processing will also see a shift in data storage solutions. Traditional databases are increasingly being replaced by distributed storage systems that can accommodate the vast amounts of unstructured data generated by modern applications. Technologies such as cloud storage, object storage, and NoSQL databases will become more prevalent, allowing for greater scalability and flexibility.

The efficiency of data retrieval can be modeled as:

$$E = \frac{R}{S} \qquad (50)$$

Where E is the efficiency of data retrieval, R is the rate of data retrieval, and S is the size of the dataset. As organizations adopt these new storage paradigms, they will be better equipped to manage and analyze their data in real-time.

6. Democratization of Data Analytics

Finally, the democratization of data analytics will empower non-technical users to engage with data effectively. With advancements in user interface design, natural language processing, and automated analytics tools, individuals across various

THE FUTURE OF DATA PROCESSING 129

sectors will have the ability to derive insights from data without requiring extensive technical expertise. This shift will foster a culture of data-driven decision-making, enhancing organizational agility and innovation.

The equation representing the accessibility of data analytics can be expressed as:

$$A = \frac{U}{C} \qquad (51)$$

Where A is the accessibility of data analytics, U is the usability of the tools, and C is the complexity of the underlying technology. As accessibility improves, we can expect a more data-literate workforce capable of leveraging analytics for strategic advantage.

Conclusion

In conclusion, the future of data processing is poised for transformative changes driven by advancements in technology, evolving ethical standards, and a commitment to inclusivity. Doug Cutting's legacy as a pioneer in the field of data analytics will continue to inspire future generations of developers and data scientists. By embracing these predictions and addressing the accompanying challenges, we can pave the way for a more efficient, ethical, and innovative data processing landscape.

Index

-effectiveness, 122

ability, 3, 10, 18, 21, 23, 28, 33, 39, 41, 42, 59, 61, 70, 79, 81, 89, 91, 96, 98, 99, 102, 103, 105, 108, 110, 111, 113, 123, 129
academia, 98, 100
academic, 1, 3, 9, 69, 76, 98
access, 4, 53, 67, 73, 85, 96, 106
accessibility, 71, 75, 106, 113, 129
accuracy, 12, 87, 89, 98
achievement, 111
action, 75, 110
acumen, 14
adaptability, 15, 108, 109
adaptation, 30
addition, 1, 71, 105, 114
address, 17, 18, 27, 29, 36, 41, 44, 51, 57, 60, 74, 80, 81, 83, 88, 95, 102
adeptness, 110
adoption, 19, 34–36, 39, 59, 75, 76, 98
advancement, 74, 128
advent, 1, 37, 95, 97, 112, 118
adventure, 6, 7
advertising, 101

advocacy, 115
advocate, 71, 76, 114
age, 1, 5, 85, 95, 105
agility, 76, 129
ahead, 89, 100, 102, 123
algorithm, 5, 9, 89, 128
allocation, 81, 90, 92, 115
allure, 1
ambition, 2
Amdahl, 91
amount, 25, 91, 92
analysis, 34, 36, 42, 44, 53, 99, 100, 115, 125
applicability, 17, 61
application, 28, 97
approach, 1, 6, 9, 13, 17, 19, 26, 27, 31, 36, 39, 53, 54, 57, 63, 64, 69, 73, 75, 80, 82, 89, 96, 99, 105, 107–109, 111, 113, 115, 117, 124–126
architecture, 14, 22, 29, 39–41, 47, 52, 55, 59, 65, 67, 69, 75, 80, 82, 84, 88, 89, 91, 95, 99, 101
area, 110
array, 3, 47, 54
aspect, 6, 19, 21, 31, 56, 64, 84, 90, 125

asset, 95
attendance, 44
attitude, 125
audience, 55
autonomy, 109
availability, 19, 106
avenue, 27, 114
awareness, 17

backbone, 9
backdrop, 2
balance, 55, 62–64, 87, 111–113
barrier, 97
base, 3, 35, 52, 54, 62
basis, 29
batch, 79
beacon, 35
behavior, 42, 96, 123
being, 26, 111, 128
belief, 13, 15, 16, 75, 106–109, 113, 115–117, 124
benchmark, 55
benefit, 69, 75, 99, 106
biography, 32
birth, 11, 27
blend, 11, 111
block, 33, 89, 92
blueprint, 76
boot, 125
bottleneck, 33, 90
boy, 1
brainstorming, 110
break, 105
brilliance, 72, 94
bug, 6, 106
building, 9, 20, 21, 30, 31, 125
burden, 73
business, 20, 96
buying, 97

candidate, 100
canvas, 10
capability, 33, 40, 82, 97
capacity, 28, 40
card, 43
care, 112
career, 1, 2, 4, 7, 9–11, 13, 15, 17, 18, 20, 21, 23, 71, 93, 105–107, 109
Carol Dweck, 124
case, 19, 35
chain, 117
challenge, 17, 19, 25, 29, 55, 62, 87, 92, 100, 110, 111, 125, 127
change, 107, 115
character, 2, 4
charity, 115
checksum, 89
child, 10
childhood, 1, 2
choice, 89, 119
climate, 99
cloud, 47, 102, 108, 122, 128
cluster, 31, 43, 52, 80
co, 14, 67
code, 2, 6, 9, 12, 19, 54, 56, 76, 106, 113, 124, 125
codebase, 19
collaboration, 2, 4, 7, 9, 13–16, 18, 20, 22, 23, 29, 31, 32, 55, 56, 58, 71–75, 77, 94, 99, 100, 106, 108–111, 113, 114, 118, 121, 124, 126
collection, 44
college, 8, 9
columnar, 92
combination, 7, 9, 13, 69, 89, 102, 106

Index

combiner, 92
commerce, 42
commitment, 9, 13, 15, 19, 20, 29, 31, 73, 76, 77, 89, 99, 106, 107, 109, 111, 113–115, 118, 121, 125, 129
commodity, 28
communication, 3, 71, 74, 110, 111
community, 2, 6–8, 13–15, 17–23, 29, 31, 34–36, 44, 53–58, 62–64, 67, 71, 73, 75–77, 87, 94, 99, 102, 106, 108, 110, 111, 113–115, 118, 124–126
company, 33, 36, 43, 81, 123
compatibility, 17, 55
competition, 47, 49, 102
complexity, 12, 61, 89, 98, 102, 127
compliance, 63, 89
component, 99
compression, 92
computation, 33, 90
computer, 1–3, 5, 10, 99, 105, 106
computing, 1, 2, 5–7, 11, 13, 15–17, 20, 26, 27, 47, 93, 94, 99, 100, 105, 106, 108, 123, 128
concept, 6, 12, 13, 26, 33, 90, 95, 124
concern, 62
conclusion, 4, 7, 9, 11, 17, 20, 23, 29, 36, 47, 49, 56, 58, 64, 74, 77, 96, 98, 100, 102, 111, 113, 118, 123, 126, 129
conference, 69, 113
confidence, 125, 126
configuration, 92
conflict, 110
confluence, 2, 27, 29
confusion, 19
congestion, 33
connection, 13, 125
connectivity, 112
consent, 86
consideration, 62
consistency, 87
consumer, 96
consumption, 117
content, 9, 17, 69
contention, 92
context, 40, 56, 62, 85
contrast, 33
contribution, 75, 98
control, 6, 55–58
conversion, 42
coordination, 55
core, 8, 29, 40, 44, 67, 75, 85, 90, 95, 99, 103
cornerstone, 2, 4, 18, 32, 37, 39, 44, 54, 59, 67, 75, 89, 98, 109, 123
corruption, 85
cost, 26, 27, 76, 122
courage, 11
craft, 107
crawler, 9, 28, 31, 67, 68
crawling, 9, 14, 67, 69
creation, 2, 11, 15, 18, 73
creativity, 1, 2, 4, 7, 9–12, 56, 106, 110, 113, 125
credibility, 55
credit, 43
crisis, 115
crucible, 13
cryptography, 128
culmination, 11
culture, 13, 19, 36, 73–75, 109, 111, 112, 115, 121, 129

curiosity, 1, 2, 5, 7, 105, 107, 124
curricula, 98, 100, 125
curriculum, 4
customer, 42, 43, 81, 96, 97, 117, 123
cycle, 76

damage, 115
dance, 62
data, 3–18, 20, 25–29, 31–39, 41–44, 46, 47, 49–55, 58–61, 64, 67, 69–73, 75–77, 79–103, 107, 110, 111, 113, 115–121, 123–129
database, 3, 8, 25, 53
dataset, 31
date, 100
day, 25
debugging, 6
decision, 7, 36, 43, 44, 47, 54, 55, 61, 73, 75, 95, 96, 100, 115, 129
dedication, 4, 94, 107, 109, 111, 124
delivery, 99, 117
deluge, 25, 26, 97
demand, 27, 44, 100, 102
democratization, 97, 118, 128
denominator, 10
deployment, 102
design, 3, 7, 88, 128
detection, 43, 98
developer, 31
development, 3, 6, 7, 9, 12–15, 17–22, 27, 28, 30, 32, 34, 36, 55, 56, 58, 61, 62, 64, 67, 68, 71, 74, 76, 93, 95, 96, 98–100, 105, 106, 109, 110, 113, 125

diagram, 52, 53, 107
difficulty, 102
direction, 74, 110
disaster, 115
discipline, 98
discovery, 98
disk, 92
disparity, 63
distribution, 16, 51, 52
diversity, 67, 76, 82, 126
documentation, 19, 31
domain, 66
dominance, 48
Doug, 1, 2, 5–15, 21, 28, 29, 72, 75–77, 105–113
Doug combats, 112
Doug Cutting, 1, 2, 5, 10, 11, 15, 16, 18–22, 27, 29–32, 37, 54, 62–64, 67, 71–74, 87, 93, 110, 111, 113, 115, 118, 123, 124, 126
Doug Cutting's, 2, 4, 7, 9, 11, 13, 15, 17, 18, 20–23, 64, 67, 69, 72–77, 89, 94, 105–107, 109, 111, 113, 115, 118, 121, 124–126, 129
drop, 80
duality, 62
dynamic, 12, 34, 103

e, 42
ease, 65
economy, 82
ecosystem, 14, 19, 29, 31, 35, 44, 46, 47, 49, 53, 54, 56, 57, 61, 64, 70, 72, 73, 75, 95–97, 102, 110, 114, 124
edge, 63, 82, 96

Index 135

education, 2–4, 11, 19, 20, 76, 77, 105, 106, 113, 115, 121, 125
effect, 107
effectiveness, 39, 44, 46, 73, 122
efficiency, 12, 26, 33, 43, 44, 52, 60, 89, 90, 97, 100, 115, 117, 128
effort, 76, 100, 108
emergence, 27, 42, 48, 95, 98
emphasis, 19
empowerment, 109, 111, 113
encoding, 92
encouragement, 2
endeavor, 7, 29, 34
engagement, 6, 15, 18, 20, 44, 54, 56, 62, 64, 75, 114, 115, 118
engine, 7, 12, 17, 108
enhancement, 53
enjoyment, 113
ensure, 67, 79, 86, 87, 93, 98
enterprise, 79, 80, 82
entrepreneurship, 96
entry, 96, 97
environment, 1, 2, 12, 34, 35, 74, 75, 87, 108–110, 124, 126
equation, 7, 10–12, 29, 42, 51, 52, 60, 62, 66, 98, 100, 102, 105, 106, 108, 114, 115, 122, 127, 129
equilibrium, 111
era, 10, 15, 27
essence, 9, 11, 108
ethic, 107, 109
ethos, 15, 75, 106, 115, 124
event, 11, 89
evolution, 18, 23, 35, 37, 47, 49, 51, 52, 56, 58, 62, 64, 67, 69, 73, 77, 94, 96, 100, 102, 103, 108, 126
example, 3, 6, 17, 20, 28, 33, 74, 89, 96–99, 102, 108, 110, 111, 115, 117, 123–125
excellence, 107
exception, 1, 12, 96
execution, 92
expanse, 67
expansion, 75
experience, 2, 6–8, 13, 15, 18, 42, 56, 71, 125
experiment, 35, 106
experimentation, 2, 109, 124
expertise, 2, 18, 19, 31, 72, 75, 129
exploration, 2, 17
explosion, 25, 29
exposure, 2, 3, 7, 13, 55, 106

face, 4, 79, 82, 108, 125
facet, 75
faceting, 69
factor, 39, 82, 91, 108
faculty, 69
failure, 12, 13, 62, 89, 106
family, 2, 105, 113
fascination, 1, 5, 106
father, 1, 105
fatigue, 112
fault, 27, 31
feature, 33, 63, 99
feedback, 15, 18, 29, 31, 53, 110
field, 2, 7, 9, 10, 16, 93, 94, 98, 103, 105, 106, 113, 117, 126, 129
figure, 118
file, 89
filtering, 69
finance, 36, 43, 53, 75, 95

flexibility, 14, 33, 34, 42, 47, 59, 69, 80, 100, 113, 128
flourish, 108
flow, 35, 73, 119
focus, 3, 29, 87, 102, 115, 120
foray, 7, 17
force, 19, 20, 61, 96, 115
forefront, 41, 67, 93
foresight, 62, 89
form, 9, 33
format, 33, 84
formula, 52, 60
foster, 31, 87, 109, 114, 129
foundation, 5, 9, 10, 15, 29, 105
fragmentation, 17, 19, 55
framework, 18, 19, 27–29, 31, 32, 34, 42, 44, 52, 54, 59, 61, 64, 67, 72, 79, 82, 85, 87, 95, 97, 98, 100, 101, 110
fraud, 43, 98
frequency, 114
fruition, 12
frustration, 12
fuel, 5, 117
fulfillment, 113
function, 66, 101
functionality, 12, 18, 35, 61, 62
future, 1, 2, 7, 9, 11, 13, 15–17, 20, 23, 32, 37, 50, 56, 64, 67, 69, 76, 77, 87, 90, 94, 96–98, 100, 102, 103, 106, 109, 111, 115, 118, 121, 123–126, 128, 129

game, 6, 7
generation, 20, 56, 71, 76, 77, 100, 103, 110, 120, 121, 124–126
genomic, 99

giant, 42, 81
Git, 57
globe, 20
goal, 62, 90
good, 106, 114, 115
governance, 34, 54–56, 74, 98
graduation, 55
groundbreaking, 2, 9, 10, 13, 62, 102
groundwork, 1, 2, 7, 13, 16, 17, 29, 32, 37, 69, 87, 106, 110, 115
group, 3, 21, 110
Grover, 128
growth, 6, 12, 25, 37, 39, 44, 68, 73, 76, 93, 97, 114, 115, 124, 126
guidance, 36, 106, 110, 125
guide, 20, 64
guiding, 2, 56, 77, 90, 105, 106, 110, 111, 126

Hadoop, 60, 90, 92, 95, 100
hallmark, 110
hand, 85
handling, 37, 82, 86, 90, 101
hardware, 28
hashing, 89
head, 11
health, 113, 115, 117
healthcare, 36, 53, 75, 95, 96, 99, 117
heart, 44, 109
helm, 123
heterogeneity, 82, 84
history, 97, 105
home, 1
household, 1, 5

idea, 13, 34, 71, 90

Index

ideal, 100
identity, 2, 107
imagination, 7
impact, 2, 4, 6, 20, 32, 36, 42, 47, 55, 67, 72–76, 97, 98, 102, 111, 114, 115, 125
implementation, 28, 29, 86
importance, 3, 6, 9, 11, 13–16, 20, 23, 54, 56, 64, 71, 74, 75, 93, 100, 105, 106, 109–114, 117, 124, 125
improvement, 18, 34, 52, 53, 60
inception, 27, 34, 51, 67, 94, 100
inclusion, 98, 124, 126
inclusivity, 52, 76, 109, 129
increase, 25, 40, 42
indexing, 15, 17, 65, 69
individual, 21, 72, 117
industry, 2, 4, 9, 11, 13, 15, 16, 18, 20, 23, 32, 36, 55, 58, 72–74, 76, 87, 94–96, 98, 99, 106–109, 111–113, 115, 125, 126
influence, 2, 16, 18, 20, 58, 72–74, 76, 77, 94–96, 98, 100, 101, 103, 105, 107, 115, 124, 126
influx, 74
information, 8, 17, 64, 67, 85, 87, 97, 106, 125
infrastructure, 47, 55
ingestion, 119
initiative, 22, 76
innovation, 2, 3, 7, 9–13, 15, 16, 18, 20, 27, 29, 31, 34, 35, 37, 44, 47, 56, 61–64, 72–77, 82, 87, 93, 94, 96, 98, 106, 107, 109, 111–114, 118, 124, 126, 129
innovator, 2, 10, 11, 107
input, 110
inquiry, 1
inspiration, 29, 106
instability, 62
instance, 3, 5, 6, 18, 33, 42, 63, 69, 73, 75, 86, 92, 95, 97, 99, 101, 102, 107, 108, 112, 113, 117, 124–126
institution, 3, 63, 98
integration, 17, 19, 53, 55, 59, 61, 97, 98, 102
integrity, 74, 87–89, 125
intellect, 1, 2, 10
intelligence, 3, 21, 96, 102, 110
interaction, 33
interconnectedness, 106
interest, 5–8, 105
interface, 119, 128
internet, 9, 11, 12, 25, 67, 69
interoperability, 17, 59
interplay, 101
intersection, 27, 85, 106
intervention, 44
introduction, 5, 37, 51, 52, 62, 70, 105
inventory, 96, 97
investment, 36
involvement, 17, 19, 21, 71, 76, 114, 119
issue, 19, 55, 112
iteration, 18

Java, 6, 52
job, 4, 11–13
journey, 2, 4, 7, 9–11, 13, 15, 16, 18, 20, 27, 29, 34, 37, 51, 55, 56, 58, 64, 67, 72, 76, 87,

94, 103, 105, 112, 113,
123, 125
joy, 2

key, 5, 15, 21, 30, 44, 51, 75, 87, 90,
101, 109, 126
knowledge, 2–4, 6, 13, 15, 19, 20,
31, 36, 73, 75, 76, 99, 105,
106, 111, 124, 125

landscape, 5, 9, 13, 14, 16, 17, 29,
32, 36, 47, 50, 51, 54–56,
58, 61, 67, 72, 74, 77, 79,
84, 89, 94, 96, 97, 100,
102, 103, 108, 115, 118,
121, 123, 124, 126, 129
language, 7, 52, 105, 128
latency, 90
layer, 102
leader, 14, 72
leadership, 109–111
learning, 1, 2, 4, 7, 12, 43, 70, 71, 79,
96–99, 102, 105, 106, 108,
109, 123, 124
legacy, 54, 56, 75–77, 94, 96,
100–102, 109, 115, 126,
129
lesson, 23
level, 6, 79, 82, 97, 110, 114
leverage, 42, 47, 52, 73, 88, 90, 96,
97, 117
leveraging, 82, 84, 87, 93, 100, 114,
128
library, 64, 67, 108
licensing, 73, 75
life, 4, 105, 111–113
lifecycle, 85, 87
light, 77, 111, 126
likelihood, 92

line, 113
literacy, 120
locality, 33, 90, 92
log, 89
logging, 89
logistic, 42
love, 1
Lucene, 14, 15, 64, 66, 67, 75, 108,
111

machine, 16, 43, 70, 79, 96–98, 102,
108, 123
mailing, 55, 110
maintenance, 43
making, 7, 23, 36, 43, 44, 47, 54, 55,
61, 73, 95–97, 100, 115,
129
management, 6, 8, 17, 44, 54, 80, 82,
88, 90, 96, 97, 102, 110,
111, 115, 117
manipulation, 6, 97
manner, 99
map, 92
mapper, 92
mark, 77, 100, 109
market, 81
marketing, 42, 96, 123
matter, 111
maturity, 36
maze, 6
mb, 92
means, 5, 33, 106
measure, 115
mechanism, 89
media, 25, 33, 37, 97, 99
medicine, 99
memory, 6, 52, 92
mentorship, 2, 4, 71, 76, 110, 111,
125, 126

method, 5
methodology, 109, 117
metric, 98
milestone, 69
mind, 39, 79, 112
mindset, 1, 7, 9, 12, 76, 108, 124, 126
mini, 92
mining, 99
mismatch, 89
model, 16, 27, 28, 30, 34, 39, 42–44, 53–56, 73, 75, 79, 98, 113, 124, 127
moment, 37
momentum, 47, 106
monitoring, 115
motion, 8
move, 32, 33, 75, 103
movement, 2, 6, 9, 16, 17, 20, 75, 77, 106, 110, 114
myriad, 47, 105

name, 93
narrative, 15, 72, 87
nature, 12, 19, 22, 53, 54, 57, 69, 96, 107, 113
necessity, 11, 27, 29, 62
need, 10, 12, 14–17, 25–27, 30, 35, 37, 47, 49, 55, 67, 77, 82, 90, 102, 118, 125
negotiation, 110
network, 4, 21, 33, 38, 43, 71, 90, 92
networking, 13, 20, 21, 23
NiFi, 119
node, 33
non, 128
norm, 96
notion, 5
number, 52, 55, 92, 114

Nutch, 15, 111

object, 128
obligation, 113
obsolescence, 96
obstacle, 107
on, 1–4, 6, 7, 9, 11–13, 15–20, 27–30, 32–34, 36, 41–44, 47, 52, 55, 62, 63, 67, 69, 71, 72, 75, 77, 80, 85, 87, 92, 94, 96–103, 105, 107, 109–113, 115, 118, 120, 124–126
one, 2, 19, 26, 34, 41, 82, 114
operation, 9
opportunity, 4, 12, 106, 113
optimization, 43, 90–93, 128
option, 53
organization, 82, 125
origin, 84
original, 33, 52, 89
other, 13, 56, 59, 61, 69, 72, 77, 85, 93
overwork, 112
ownership, 19, 54, 109

pace, 15, 16, 25, 67
paradigm, 16, 17, 20, 28, 95
parallel, 26, 90–92
participant, 114
participation, 18, 108, 126
partitioning, 91
partnership, 72
passion, 2, 3, 5, 7, 10, 106, 107, 118
path, 13, 19
patient, 96, 99, 117
perception, 73

performance, 6, 18, 40, 44, 47, 51–53, 55, 60, 62, 80, 90–93, 98, 122, 127
period, 13, 17, 55, 105
perseverance, 4, 15, 106, 107, 109
persistence, 10
person, 2
personnel, 102
perspective, 107
phase, 28, 55
phenomenon, 95
philanthropic, 106, 113, 115
philanthropy, 113, 114
philosophy, 16, 32, 73, 75, 109, 124
physicist, 1
physics, 1, 7, 8
pioneer, 7, 109, 124, 129
planning, 55, 62
platform, 18, 29, 55, 69, 98
point, 16, 70, 113
pool, 18
popularity, 55
portion, 68
position, 8, 36, 44, 55, 123
positive, 107, 115
possibility, 2
potential, 17, 26, 28, 35, 36, 39, 47, 62, 68, 76, 90, 98, 107, 117, 121, 123, 126, 128
power, 15, 20, 27, 32, 36, 42, 56, 61, 66, 69, 74, 75, 82, 87, 93, 99, 109, 113, 115, 118, 121, 124
precedent, 124
predictability, 62
pressure, 113
principle, 20, 90, 105, 110
privacy, 85–87, 125, 127
problem, 5–7, 9–13, 17, 22, 31, 41, 71, 105, 107–110, 113, 124–126
process, 3, 4, 7, 12, 16, 20, 25, 27–29, 31, 32, 36, 43, 52, 54, 59, 70, 79, 82, 91, 95, 96, 98, 99, 123
processing, 9, 11, 15–17, 20, 25–29, 31–37, 39, 41, 42, 44, 47, 49–55, 59, 62, 64, 69, 70, 72, 73, 75, 77, 79–82, 84–87, 89–103, 107, 110, 111, 113, 115, 118, 121, 123–126, 128, 129
product, 12, 107
professional, 4, 10, 11, 17, 71, 85, 100, 111
professor, 105
proficiency, 8
program, 3, 7, 76
programmer, 2, 13, 107
programming, 1–9, 13, 27, 39, 52, 75, 76, 97, 105, 106, 124–126
progress, 19, 20, 74
project, 8, 9, 12, 14, 17–19, 22, 31, 34, 54, 55, 58, 67, 74–76, 108, 110, 119, 124, 125
proliferation, 16
protection, 87
prototype, 31
prowess, 12, 13
pseudocode, 9
psychologist, 124
public, 73, 99, 115
purchase, 97
purchasing, 96, 117, 123
purpose, 109
pursuit, 11, 32, 105, 107

Index

quality, 19, 54, 56, 98, 101, 114, 118
quantum, 128
querying, 53, 95, 97
quest, 10

range, 51, 108, 124, 126
read, 33, 89, 92
reality, 11
realm, 2, 6, 7, 13, 20, 34, 39, 56, 62, 65, 68, 74, 82, 85, 87, 94, 109, 115, 117, 125
reasoning, 105
recognition, 34–36, 74, 76, 93, 94
reduce, 12, 81, 91, 92, 100
reducer, 92
regression, 42
relationship, 62, 72, 127
release, 54, 75
relevance, 50, 74, 102
reliability, 55, 62, 87–89, 98
reliance, 19
reminder, 113, 115
replica, 33, 89
replication, 33, 89
report, 19, 25
reputation, 14
requirement, 86
research, 27–29, 36, 98–100
resilience, 4, 124
resolution, 110
resolve, 107
resource, 80, 81, 90, 92, 115, 122
response, 35, 47, 67, 103, 115
responsibility, 87, 106, 126
rest, 112
result, 16, 19, 75, 81, 97, 110
retail, 36, 42, 81, 95–97, 117, 123
retrieval, 64, 67, 128
revolution, 49, 93, 102

right, 53
rigor, 105
rise, 16, 47, 61, 97, 101, 102
risk, 44, 96, 117
robustness, 62
role, 2, 10, 12, 13, 18, 35, 44, 56, 59, 61, 67, 71, 72, 76, 95, 98, 100–102, 105–107, 109, 115, 123, 125
rollout, 63
routing, 119

s, 1–23, 28, 29, 31–36, 39–44, 48, 51–53, 55, 56, 58, 59, 61, 64–67, 69, 71–77, 84, 89, 91, 92, 94–100, 102, 105–115, 117–119, 121, 123–126, 128, 129
salting, 91
satisfaction, 43, 97, 117
saving, 117
scalability, 11, 15, 18, 27, 31, 39–42, 47, 55, 79, 80, 82, 100, 124, 128
scale, 17, 26, 27, 33, 39, 41, 79, 80, 99, 100
scaling, 107, 124
scenario, 33
scheduling, 52
schema, 33
school, 7
science, 1, 3, 5, 10, 70, 76, 97–99, 105
scoring, 66
scripting, 35, 73
scrutiny, 85
search, 12, 15, 17, 64–69, 108, 128
section, 42, 44, 59, 65, 75, 85, 87, 90, 98

sector, 4, 42, 43, 96, 117
security, 53, 54, 85–87, 107, 118, 125
self, 112
sense, 2, 19, 54, 106, 126
sentiment, 99
serialization, 60
series, 7, 13
set, 3, 5, 11, 13, 17, 32, 55, 74, 89, 105, 124, 125
setback, 106, 124
setting, 9, 27, 113
sharing, 2, 19, 20, 36, 73, 99, 106, 124, 125
shift, 16, 20, 73, 95, 96, 101, 128, 129
significance, 5, 15, 23, 37, 125
Silicon Valley, 2
simulation, 8
size, 60
skew, 91
skill, 3, 76, 105
society, 106, 115, 125
software, 3, 9, 12–17, 21, 56, 58, 62, 64, 67, 71, 73, 74, 77, 105, 106, 109, 114
solution, 11, 22, 25–27, 30, 37, 42, 44, 53, 55, 67, 72, 107
solving, 5–7, 9–13, 29, 31, 71, 76, 105, 107–110, 113, 124–126
source, 2, 6, 8, 9, 13–21, 23, 29, 31, 32, 34–36, 44, 53–57, 59, 62, 64, 67, 69, 71–77, 79, 93, 94, 96, 99, 100, 106–111, 113–115, 118, 124, 126
space, 92, 109
spark, 1

speed, 11, 12, 27, 81, 90, 92, 100
speedup, 91, 128
spirit, 2, 9–11, 18, 20, 29, 44, 56, 72, 75, 77, 108, 114, 124
stability, 55, 56, 62–64
stage, 9, 11, 17, 27, 110
standard, 89
startup, 12, 13, 63
state, 89
status, 36, 54
step, 110, 113
stone, 13
storage, 12, 14, 27, 29, 32, 37, 39, 44, 54, 59, 79, 92, 95, 100, 102, 128
store, 8, 29, 33, 38, 75, 79, 99
story, 34, 72, 74
strategy, 33, 44, 58, 63
stress, 112
structure, 33
student, 43, 125
style, 109–111
subject, 5
subsection, 2, 16, 18, 29, 51, 56, 124
subset, 92
success, 13–15, 17, 19, 20, 22, 23, 36, 42, 54, 62, 74, 76, 82, 89, 93, 108, 109, 111, 113, 115, 118
suite, 84
summary, 2, 13, 27, 32, 39, 54, 61, 67, 93, 106, 109, 115, 121
supply, 117
support, 21, 34, 36, 52, 67, 102, 125, 126
sustainability, 76, 110, 117
synergy, 10, 12, 102, 105
system, 8, 40, 55, 57, 62, 82, 88, 89, 126

Index

t, 108
tale, 10
talent, 18, 126
tapestry, 1
task, 91, 92
team, 10, 12, 19, 28, 30, 31, 54, 72, 87, 109, 110, 124
teamwork, 3, 12, 20, 23, 110, 124
tech, 2, 4, 9–11, 13, 15–18, 20, 23, 32, 36, 55, 72–75, 87, 94, 96, 98, 100, 106–115, 118, 125, 126
technology, 1–5, 7, 9, 12, 13, 15, 16, 18, 20, 23, 29, 32, 36, 37, 39, 54, 62, 64, 73, 75–77, 82, 94, 95, 100, 105–107, 109, 111–115, 123–126, 129
temptation, 112
term, 25
test, 8, 31
testament, 17, 20, 32, 36, 67, 74, 75, 94, 109, 113, 115
testing, 64
text, 6, 7
The San Francisco Bay Area, 2
theft, 85
theory, 3, 105, 109, 110
thinker, 4
thinking, 2, 5, 8, 9, 67, 105
thought, 14, 99
throughput, 90
time, 8, 12, 13, 17, 19, 33, 34, 36, 43, 49, 53, 60, 68, 69, 75, 79, 81, 91, 98, 100, 102, 110–113
today, 4, 74, 125
tolerance, 27, 31

tool, 5, 9, 53, 61, 69, 99, 106, 123, 125
top, 52, 69
track, 56
tracking, 55
traction, 12, 19, 36, 54, 74
traffic, 92
train, 98, 108
training, 79, 98
trajectory, 2, 17, 72, 74
transaction, 43, 81, 98
transfer, 76, 90
transformation, 33, 51
transition, 6
transparency, 15, 56, 71, 75, 106, 110, 124
transportation, 117
triad, 85
trip, 113
trust, 110
Tuckman, 110
tuning, 82, 92
turn, 113
turning, 16, 70
type, 82

understanding, 3, 6, 8, 12, 15, 82, 87, 92, 99, 105, 106, 111–113, 115
underutilization, 91
unit, 33
universe, 105
university, 43, 69, 71
update, 8
usability, 47, 53, 102
use, 19, 22, 36, 42, 67, 68, 89, 98
user, 6, 12, 33, 35, 49, 52–54, 62, 63, 101, 102, 119, 125, 128
utility, 127

utilization, 52, 90, 122

vacation, 113
value, 2, 25, 73, 76, 101, 106, 124
variety, 25, 27, 32, 61, 79, 95, 101
velocity, 8, 25, 79, 95
venture, 119
versatility, 61, 66
version, 17, 55–58
versioning, 58, 64
viability, 14, 17, 28
view, 124
vigilance, 87
visibility, 55
vision, 13, 19, 20, 29, 32, 67, 69, 72, 74, 106, 115, 117, 118, 124
visionary, 9, 20, 87, 94, 107, 111, 115, 126
volume, 11, 25, 61, 67, 79, 89, 95, 98, 101, 127

warehousing, 35, 73, 102
way, 1, 4, 11, 15, 16, 18, 27, 29, 32, 36, 61, 64, 69, 87, 94, 96, 108, 129
web, 9, 14, 15, 17, 28, 31, 33, 67–69
whole, 106, 125
willingness, 13, 108
work, 2, 3, 13, 15–18, 44, 72, 75–77, 105, 107, 109, 111–113, 115, 121, 124, 125
workload, 40, 80, 92
world, 1–3, 5, 7, 10–12, 14, 17, 19, 20, 28, 29, 31, 35, 44, 46, 53, 56, 62, 64, 73, 75, 77, 87, 93, 96, 99, 105–107, 109, 111, 115, 117, 120, 123, 125, 126

Milton Keynes UK
Ingram Content Group UK Ltd.
UKHW020318021124
450424UK00013B/1318